Being and Awesomeness:
Get Rad, Stay Rad

_____

Tiffany Zlatich Tuttle, Psy.D

_____

PEGASUS BOOKS

Pegasus Books
3338 San Marino Ave
San Jose, CA 95127
www.pegasusbooks.net

First Edition: July 2015

Published in North America by Pegasus Books. For information, please contact Pegasus Books c/o Christopher Moebs, 3338 San Marino Ave, San Jose, CA 95127.

This book is a work of non-fiction. Any resemblance to actual persons, living or dead, events, or locales is entirely coincidental.

Library of Congress Cataloguing-In-Publication Data
Tiffany Zlatich Tuttle
Being and Awesomeness/Tiffany Zlatich Tuttle 1st ed
p. cm.
Library of Congress Control Number: 2015946433
ISBN – 978-1-941859-33-9

1. PSYCHOLOGY / General. 2. SELF-HELP / Personal Growth / General. 3. HUMOR / General. 4. PSYCHOLOGY / Psychotherapy / Counseling. 5. EDUCATION / Educational Psychology. 6. PSYCHOLOGY / Personality.

10 9 8 7 6 5 4 3 2 1

Comments about *Being and Awesomeness* and requests for additional copies, book club rates and author speaking appearances may be addressed to Tiffany Zlatich Tuttle or Pegasus Books c/o Christopher Moebs, 3338 San Marino Ave, San Jose, CA, 95127, or you can send your comments and requests via e-mail to cmoebs@pegasusbooks.net.

Also available as an eBook from Internet retailers and from Pegasus Books

Printed in the United States of America

To you.

If there's a break in any part of yourself, it means there's room for light to shine in and make you better. We all need a little healing sometimes.

ACKNOWLEDGMENTS

Thank you to anyone who hasn't been a jerk to me. To my family—living, or living in spirit, true blue friends, and loving animal companions, you are everything to me.

Special thanks to Malo Konjche for making the music that soothes my soul and rocks my heart. And to Spazz Happy Line Design for being my creative outlet when I had writer's block. These both kept me from eating my hair and climbing the walls.

Last, for Jeff Tuttle, you are forever my boy. Thank you for ruling.

Being and Awesomeness: Get Rad, Stay Rad is the first book by clinical psychologist **Dr. Tiffany Tuttle.** In her attempt to take the "sigh" out of psychology, Dr. Tuttle breathes new life into the field by celebrating self-help. She is unapologetic about her sense of humor and uses it to keep readers engaged so they can learn how to enhance their quality of life. Coming to terms with the past, understanding how early attachments influence today's behavior, conquering depression and anxiety, increasing self-awareness, finding ways to boost motivation and actually follow through on making positive changes are among the topics Dr. Tuttle examines in this useful, surprisingly wise handbook.

BEING and AWESOMENESS:
Get Rad, Stay Rad

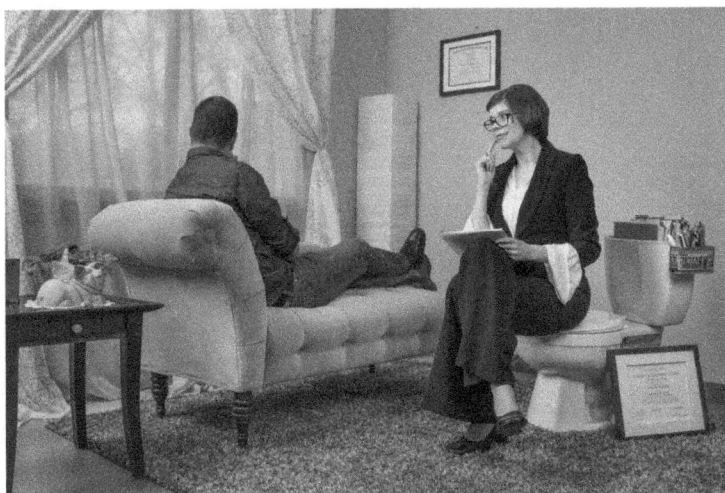

Contents

Part III: Change

About the Author

Tiffany Tuttle wants to ignite personal growth on a mass level while simultaneously tickling the funny bone that many (like her) keep inside.

Tiffany, Tiff Tuttle, or Tiff Tutts, as her friends call her, earned her doctorate in clinical psychology in 2008 and facilitates therapy for a living. Dr. Tuttle presents with signs of anxiety and exhibits some functional neurotic personality traits, including talking rapidly when nervous and smiling frequently. Dr. Tuttle also displays catastrophizing cognitive distortions with primary ruminations that loved ones will become terminally ill or otherwise perish in disturbing ways. These feelings likely stem from the death of her father to brain cancer when she was 14. Dr. Tuttle reportedly receives an "amazing" amount of support from her extended family and network of friends. She also acknowledges the benefits of the long and loving relationship she shares with her husband, a partnership formed at age 21, adding, "He makes me laugh every day, and he's one handsome fella! Not a bad deal."

Tiffany's prognosis seems hopeful, as she displays positive core strengths that include a lack of rigidity in her appraisal style, a continued willingness to grow, and the ability to laugh at herself.

Dr. Tuttle appears capable of accepting factors she cannot change and displays a healthy propensity to experience a range of emotions, i.e., she seems to be mindful of her feelings and responds openly to receiving them. She displays a somewhat unusual sense of humor that is at once foul yet gentle, adding that she has been dubbed "a combination of Sarah Silverman and Don Rickles," a compliment she considers a badge of honor.

Dr. Tuttle's working diagnosis is Anxiety Disorder Not Otherwise Specified. She professes to being committed to the therapeutic process and is poised to reap the benefits that psychotherapy has to offer.

Introduction

Hi. My name is Tiffany and I'm pretty sure I like you. If you don't punch babies or kick dogs, then we will probably get along. The preceding vignette was an introduction of sorts; I'm a clinical psychologist and I write stuff like this all the time for my clients. This is how I would assess myself.

I wanted to write this book because it would let me combine three of my favorite hobbies: 1) helping others, 2) being nice, and 3) trying to get some laughs. The result is one giant ball of awesomeness—or to be specific, the book you're reading. I'm formally trained as a clinical psychologist, and I promise I have a bunch of degrees if you need evidence. In order to earn your respect though, I'll give you a little history about me so you can check me out and size me up. I mean, if you decide to go on this journey to awesomeness with me, you have to trust me, right? Okay, so about me . . .

As a kid I was a total spazz, and I would play from sunup to sundown. I did well in school, but as soon as the bell rang I was out the door and ready to ride bikes and/or jump off/out anything, including second-story windows. I didn't care how old you were or what kind of clothes you wore. I didn't care what color or nationality you were. It didn't matter what kind of house you lived in, whether you had two parents or one or lived with your aunt and uncle or grandparents. That stuff was irrelevant. The only criterion for being my friend was *Be Nice*.

I stuck up for the so-called dorks and befriended the unpopular kids. As far back as I can remember, my behavior was guided by this beautifully simple notion: treat others the way you want to be treated. That's not to say I wouldn't stick it to the occasional bully. I once put a tack on a kid's seat because he wouldn't stop picking on this little guy. He sat on it, screamed, and had blood-butt stains on the back of his khakis for the rest of the day (sorry/notsorry).[1,2]

---

[1] Don't judge me. Remember that I was just a kid and unaware of my conflicting ideologies.
[2] Bullies can totally suck it.

I've always been drawn to individuals who get the short end of the stick—people who struggle, who have not always been fed with a silver spoon, who have been labeled different, weird, or misfit. These were the kids I gravitated toward. Not because there's anything wrong with being privileged, but because I felt that the ones who had struggles needed more love. So early on, I saw there was a need for me to be nice to the people that had difficulty, the kids who were made fun of, the ones whose parents couldn't afford to buy them name-brand clothes, the ones who had some physical or mental disorder that made them "special."

I found that being nice to these folks was effortless, because in my mind, these guys and girls had a need for social acceptance and a desire to be liked by others, as we all do, and for whatever reason, they were being deprived of that need and desire. Seeing this deprivation gave me the green light to help. This is some next-level shit going on in my elementary-school brain, but it's what happened.

My inclinations are not altruistic by any means, either. I feel a profound sense of validation and meaning when I am nice to someone and I am able to cheer them up, or make them laugh, or make them feel good about themselves. Those good feelings reinforced my drive to help and be friendly, and as I got older, led me to my dream career as a psychologist.

I've learned that people who seek psychotherapy do so because they need help and support. I have been training for this since I was five. So whether you have dabbled in therapy or not, if you need help and support in your life, or if you're just curious about learning more about yourself, this is the right book for you. My predisposition toward empathy, combined with all my clinical training, has taught me some things that I think will benefit you. Your life is what matters here, and if you allow these words, juiced from my brain lemons, to do their job, you can learn some things—preferably a lot of things—to make your life better.

This book is for people who want to learn more about the internal workings of their minds and for those who may be interested in therapy, psychotherapy, or counseling. You don't have to have a history of getting therapy to benefit from this book, but it's cool if you do. Maybe you've tried therapy and are looking for ways to supplement it—or maybe you don't give a shit about therapy and you just want to learn about yourself. It's-all-good. No matter how you slice this pizza, pro-therapy or not so pro-therapy, if you're curious about you, and you meet the following five criteria, this book is up your alley.

- Want to become more self-aware
- Want to learn better coping skills
- Want to improve your quality of life
- Can tolerate some jokes about butts, titties, and diarrhea
- Are between the ages of 18 and, I don't know, 120?

So, if you're up for taking a journey into the depths of your consciousness, open to positive change, AND you're not totally offended by words like shitbird, balls, and cunty tossed in for comic relief, then this is the book for you! It's about 20% potty humor and 80% legit stuff you need to know. This book is a crash course (without the crashing-down part) in learning how to be the best damn version of yourself possible.

Break it down for me, @tifftutts

Here is the simple truth: Life is not easy. It sucks nards sometimes. Horrible things happen to us, and the people we love, and sometimes all we can do is watch. Relationships that once seemed perfect get all fucked up, shat on and horrible. Sometimes we hate our jobs, hate our families, hate our childhoods, feel hopeless, feel angry, and feel overwhelmed.

There is another side to this, though, and here's what I want to help you understand: just as we have the capacity to feel all the stanky stuff mentioned above, we also have the capacity to become empowered. We have free will and can change some of the things that cause us misery. We can reframe our thinking and change our attitude, so the way we experience life is actually better. We can be more mindful of the connection between our thoughts, emotions, and behaviors.

We can learn to high five and hug our emotions—all of them, including anger, depression, and anxiety—so we can improve our coping skills. We can accept that there are some things we have no power to change, and take action to change the things we do have control over. We can let ourselves be vulnerable in the face of people who love us, and we can heal.

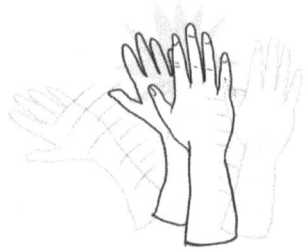

Where this book will take you

My goal is to help you understand your thoughts, your emotions, and your behavior so you can see how they shape the way you experience the world. I'll present the basics to get your biggest brain gears moving so you can apply them to your everyday life and become more of the person you want to be.

In order to understand why you are the way you are right now, we have to go back to the start, but I promise we won't get stuck talking about your childhood forever. A lot of people avoid therapy because they think it means talking about their upbringing all the damn time, but that's not going to happen here. Here, I just want to give you some information that will let you make important connections between your past and your present—AND help you resolve any unfinished business from back in the day if you have it, so you can be the you that you want to be right now.

In Part I, we're going to talk about attachment, then identify what kinds of attachments you had with the people in your life as you grew up, so you can see how they affect you today. Then we're going to sit down with two of the most prevalent issues folks in the modern world struggle with today: depression and anxiety. Knowledge is power, so a better understanding of these problems will help you cope with them in healthier ways. You'll learn how to stop negative thoughts and why it's important to make friends with feelings you don't enjoy having.

In Part II, I'll explain what self-awareness is and show you how to get/increase it so you can be more of a badass. Tips and fancy tricks for maintaining, managing, and nurturing a healthy mind will be outlined for you.

And in Part III, we'll talk about how people actually change.

This is a basic self-help book that's designed to pollinate some of your brain seeds with awesomeness so you can watch them bloom on your own time. Your life is important and you deserve happiness now.

This book will help you

- be more aware of why you think the way you do,
- understand how your thoughts influence your behavior,
- stop negative thinking from ruining your life,
- learn how to accept all of your feelings, including anxiety,
- understand how to manage your feelings and thoughts so it's easier for you to act in ways that aren't crazy nutso and promote well-being,
- recognize that you are an active agent for change in your own life,
- learn how to be successful at making the things you want to happen. . . actually happen.

If you can grasp and integrate these sexy dotted points into your life, not only will you be enlightened, you will unleash your awesome power of awesomeness. If you feel a surge in your "shit yeah, I'm rad" meter after reading this intro, then you are already on your way to getting rad and staying rad. Hooray for you! Thumbs up, smile, hug so tight I lift you off the ground, high five, wink, and five excited snaps in a row, to you from me. Let's do this.

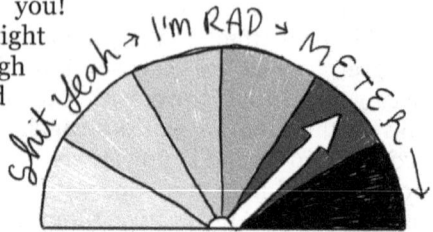

Disclaimer

Throughout this book, you will see examples of folks that I cite in order to better exemplify a point I want to bring home. It's important to note that while I'm not trying to pull a fast one on ya, these people are not real, and instead composite figures of anyone I've ever met. Friend, family, coworker, client, even parts of myself are included. Since confidentiality is central to therapy, the examples I use in no way reflect any specific client I've ever had the privilege of working with. I mean, I'd be a pretty shitty psychologist if I didn't hold that bond sacred. I do, and I'm not.

Three Ground Rules and the Four A's

Before we proceed, I'm going to outline some rules that are important to follow if you're going to get as much as you can out of this book. Whether you're prone to doing these things or not, please give them a once-over and let them sink in.

#1—Understand that no one is perfect.

Perfect => fucked => perfuct.

Being perfect is not possible. You'll just end up perfectly fucked, or as I like to call it, perfuct. Nothing in life is perfect. Trying to be perfect causes all sorts of painful maladies like anxiety, fear, depression, low self-esteem, and other sucky feelings. Holding yourself to unreasonable standards of perfection can leave you feeling demoralized and defeated. So. . . please stop doing that.

Stay with me, now: I am in no way, shape, or literary form suggesting that people cannot get better at things. We can always grow and become better human beings. What I am saying is that removing the ideal of perfection from your mind is what you need to do in order to cultivate authentic growth and glean anything positive from this here book.

So, if you have a friend, or coworker, or someone famous that you idolize and think has a perfect life, or perfect marriage, or perfect relationship with his or her partner, parents, kids, or in-laws, I'm here to say your mind is deceiving you. Perception does not necessarily equal reality.

No one Deserves TO BE PUT ON A **PEDESTAL**

We are all equal, and we are all worthy and deserving of a happy and meaningful life. The person to which you compare yourself, or wish you were more like, shits in doo-doo city just like the rest of us. We can love, admire, and respect others (including our friends, family, and famous people), but when their persona becomes inflated in our heads to the point where we feel less than, it's time for you to take that person off the pedestal and bring them back down to planet earth.

#2—Lower your defenses and be honest with yourself.

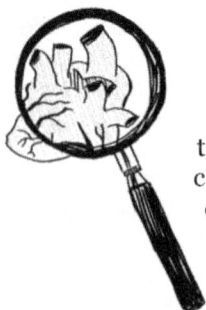

I'm asking you to take a giant magnifying glass to your heart and head so you can see what the heck is going on in there. Why make it more complicated than it needs to be? Be open to examining yourself, exploring yourself, and calling yourself out on all the shit that you do. I'll encourage you (because I like you and know that you're awesome), but you have to be truthful with yourself if you're going to get the most out of this book.

#3—Recognize that you are an active body with the capacity to change.

Throughout this book I will contend that while you are a composite of your past experiences, these experiences do not preclude you from making positive changes in your life right now.

Translation: whether you had a shit childhood, a privileged one, or one that fell somewhere in between, today, here and now as you read these words, you can take action to change the things you do not like about your life. This requires four fundamental components, or what I like to call the Four A's.

The Four A's

Awareness—Acceptance—Action—Accountability

The Four A's

→ AWARENESS
→ ACCEPTANCE
→ ACTION
→ ACCOUNTABILITY

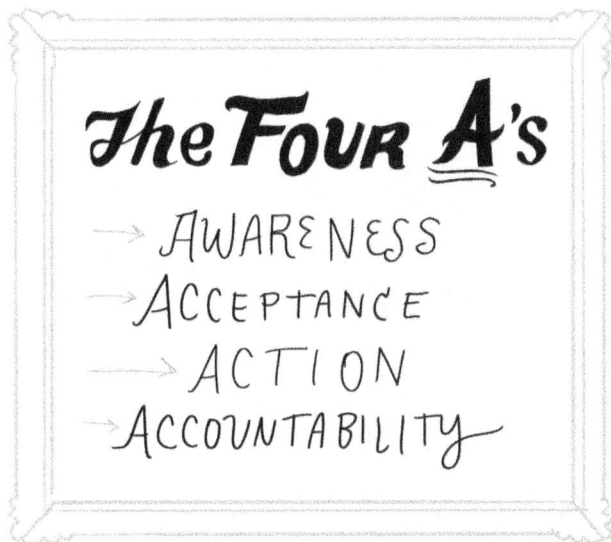

These babies are your exclusive tickets to awesomeness because they are precisely what you need to get your butt in gear and make the changes you want in your life come to fruition. Pay attention and keep these four beauties close, because in essence they are sprinkled across every page in this book.

So, why make it more complicated than it needs to be right?! Less is more, and if you can remember these three ground rules, you will be conquering the world before you know it.

PART I: BEING

Chapter 1 | Attachment theory: You really can blame some of it on other people!

In order to take a closer look at your life, where you are, and where you want to be going, you have to recall the very first attachment bond you had with someone. So we have to hop into our souped-up DeLorean or into our *Lost* helicopter or into our hot tub time machine, or use our magnificent consciousness to hit rewind and go as far back in time as that fantastic memory of yours can take you.

What's so important about attachment?

Good question! The attachments we form as babies, toddlers, and kids with the people in our immediate environments enable us to first learn about love, safety, and distress. This is of massive importance because in some capacity, love, safety, and distress are emotions swimming around all the relationships we form, whether we realize it or not. And how do we get familiar with feelings of love, safety, and distress? By experiencing them. Similarly, how can we get better at feeling love for ourself, and others? By practicing. The same goes for safety and distress. The way to get better at dealing with distress is by experiencing it, so you can then learn and practice successful strategies for managing it. Do you know who can help you work through these things when you're a youngling? A nurturing primary caregiver. That's why attachment is so critical to us. Defined as an enduring emotional bond between two people, the attachments we form early on in life set the tone for how we show love, cope with distress, and feel about ourself, and others.[1]

An attachment relationship is characterized by five things:

1. The need to maintain proximity with the person
2. The experience of distress when separated
3. The experience of joy upon reunion
4. The experience of grief when the person is dead.
5. The impact our early attachments have on our lives

The impact our early attachments have on our lives

Now, the $gazillion-dollar$ question to think about as you read on is: What did you learn from the person who was in charge of you before you had your shit together enough to deal with distress in an autonomous & healthy way?

Basic breakdown: Our relationships with our primary caregivers determine how we make sense of the world and direct our behaviors, moods, and (down the line) relationships we have with others.

So, whether it was your mother, father, mother and father, mother and mother, father and father, grandparent(s), older sibling, aunt, uncle, cousin, or a supernanny—because your parents were so loaded they had a vault filled with gold (like Scrooge McDuck)—the person that you spent the most time with as an infant and child is the person you formed your first attachment bond with, and the person who held the most critical influence over you. As you got older and began socializing with other human beings (nuclear and extended family, friends, teachers), the new attachments you formed expanded your working model of the world.

Here's an analogy: think of a railroad track. When you are born, you start off in the middle of nowhere. Now, the place you want to get to is a happy, fulfilling, meaningful destination, and your primary caregiver holds the map, whether they know it or not. (That's why so many organizations, in particular nonprofits, work so hard to educate young mothers on bonding.)

If your caregiver is consistently loving, nurturing, and encouraging, the tracks to your healthy and fulfilling future are laid with straight, even, titanium ties.

If this is not the case and your caregiver is avoidant, cold, critical, mean, unstable, abusive, inconsistent with his or her attention, and/or overindulgent and scared to let you explore your environment, you will develop an insecure attachment. If this happens, your railroad tracks will be laid with mite-infested wood on a crooked course that takes you somewhere else.

It's important to note that even if your caregiver demonstrated some of these negative characteristics some of the time, it doesn't mean they blew it. Caregivers that instill secure attachments in their children may at times be avoidant or overindulgent. There is even a concept known as "good-enough parenting" that argues that parents can compensate for their shortcomings and still be close to their kids and foster healthy attachments. So, basically, if most of the time the parents are supportive, loving, nurturing, and reliable, and if the kids are relatively resilient, then the kids will likely grow up to be healthy.

What if our attachments messed us up?

Say for instance your caregiver had gnarly mood swings; what kind of emotions do you think that would generate within you? Anxiety, fear, sadness, anger, confusion, perhaps? If so, when you first go to preschool and meet a rad kiddo you want to be friends with, you may expect him to act in a similar fashion as your caregiver. Maybe you'll try to instigate trouble or get him or her upset, because maybe you learned at home that intense emotions are normal parts of all relationships.

On the other hand, maybe you'll just keep to yourself, because you think everyone will wind up getting mad at you and push you away like your mom did.

This hypothetical situation illuminates one of many internal mental processes that may be going on when the relational groundwork between different people is being forged. Can you imagine what this kiddo would be like as an adult if he continued to behave this way?

There is good news for us adults, even if our track is made out of crappy, dank wood that has steered us to an unhappy destination where unknowing, we subconsciously settled: WE CAN CHANGE THE ROUTE. Research demonstrates that

CAREGIVERS HAVE a CRITICAL IMPACT on us, BUT THEIR INFLUENCE IS NOT SET IN STONE.

Overcoming a sucky attachment with your primary caregiver requires mindfulness and action, and we will discuss both in greater detail soon. For now, just be aware of how powerful that attachment is, and have hope that you can overcome any damage it may have caused you. Implementing awareness, acceptance, action, and accountability will gradually turn your wooden track into titanium and help steer you wherever you want.

What kind of attachment did you have with your primary caregiver?

If you want to understand yourself better, you need to identify who your primary caregiver was. Then, after you bring your experience of infancy and childhood into your awareness, take some time to identify the feelings that surface. Close your eyes, take a deep breath, and focus on your caregiver.

What comes to mind? A memory or a feeling? If a memory comes to the surface first, then you're in the thinking part of your brain, and you'll need to focus a bit more to determine what emotion is associated with it. Take your time exploring that memory to find the feeling around it. For example, if you remember being punished for "misbehaving," maybe you feel sad or mad within that memory. If you remember having been sick and having your mom by your side, maybe you feel happy and loved.

The five big emos

For those of you who need some extra umph to help you cross between the thinking and feeling parts of your brain, use these five core emotions as guides:

All of our emotions fall under one or a combination of these five babies. Everything you ever experience can fundamentally be described by the above feelings. So go on and ask yourself again: What is your first memory of that primary caregiver? What kind of person was he or she? Which of the five big emos did you feel when you were around him or her? What did you feel when you weren't around him or her? Answering these questions will help you determine the kind of attachment you had.

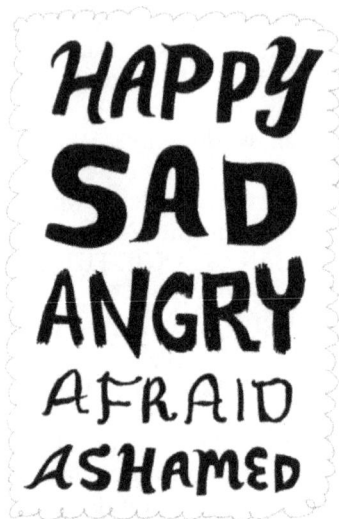

HAPPY
SAD
ANGRY
AFRAID
ASHAMED

The three main attachment patterns

In addition to the feelings that are generated as you recall your relationship with your primary caregiver, there is also something referred to as an attachment pattern, which will help you determine the type of bond you had. There are three main patterns of attachment:

- secure
- insecure-avoidant
- insecure-ambivalent[4]

Secure attachment

If you were comfortable using your caregiver as a base in order to explore your environment, then you had a secure attachment. For example, when your mom or dad left the room, you had responses like these:

- you missed him or her when you were separated from them
- you wanted contact when they came back
- you were able to be comforted once you were reunited with them
- you weren't scared to keep exploring after your reunion (i.e., you didn't cling to them with a kung-fu grip)

Your tiny little brain couldn't achieve full understanding at the time, but a secure attachment response showed that you understood you were loved. This is important because it helped you learn how to regulate your affect, which means manage your emotions, in order to deal with the stress of separation. You didn't blame or resent your parent for leaving, and you were able to return to business as usual once they came back. Cultivating a secure bond required that your caretaker was consistent with their attention and care, and that they were attuned to your needs.

Insecure-avoidant attachment

Now... with an insecure-avoidant attachment pattern, when your caregiver left the room,

- you explored the environment without looking back for them
- ignored them when they came back
- were not upset when they weren't around
- distracted yourself when they were gone

Key word here being *avoidant.* If you avoided your parent when they were or were not around, and did your own thing regardless of them, this may not mean healthy independence and autonomy. In this case, you may not have turned to your parent because you realized that you wouldn't get your needs met, so fuck it, you'd keep doing what you were doing anyway. There was no real incentive to turn to them, so why even bother?

I understand that you may not remember a precise example of your parents leaving a room that you were in, but I'm talking about generalities here. Just ask yourself how you felt when Mom or Pop was around, and how you felt when they weren't.

Insecure-ambivalent attachment

As you file through your childhood experiences, if secure or avoidant doesn't fit the bill, then perhaps you had an insecure-ambivalent attachment. An insecure-ambivalent attachment looks like this:

- you experienced distress when your caregiver left
- you were not able to be comforted when they returned
- you were wary of anyone else trying to help you

This attachment is categorized by feelings of indecision and hesitation. You want comfort and love, but get confused when an actual opportunity for them presents itself. This leaves you distressed and your need for love and safety is unfulfilled.

What attachment patterns look like in adulthood

If you still can't put your finger on the kind of attachment you had with your caretaker, it might help to go backwards from where you are right now. See if any of these look familiar.

Characteristics of adults who had secure attachments

- able to trust others and cultivate long-lasting relationships
- able to resolve conflict with partners more readily
- comfortable sharing feelings with friends and family
- more likely to have high self-esteem
- willing to seek social support in times of adversity and distress
- more likely to be an attentive parent

Characteristics of adults who had avoidant attachments

- lack emotional investment in relationships
- resistant to sharing thoughts and feelings with others
- non-empathetic toward partners who are experiencing distress
- have problems with intimacy and may prefer to avoid it
- experience little distress at the end of a relationship

Characteristics of adults who had ambivalent attachments

- concerned that their partner does not truly love them
- reluctant to become close to others
- described as being cold and distant
- become troubled and distraught when a relationship terminates

Attachment patterns affect adult relationships as long as you let them

Adults who had a secure bond of attachment with their caregiver tend to be warmer and more sensitive to others' emotions and needs. They demonstrate more positive caregiving behaviors toward their children and are more willing to work together to resolve disagreements in romantic relationships.[5]

People who have received consistent sensitive care for their needs learn to cope with distress by turning to others for support. This is an ENORMOUS (cue fireworks for emphasis here) buffer against depression and other crappy maladies like loneliness, anxiety, and rumination. These people are more open to seeking support, because when they were kids, they received constructive, emotionally focused care, during particular times of distress.

Individuals with insecure attachments, on the other hand, have a history of feeling rejected by their attachment figures. Their needs for love, attention and support may have been dismissed or ignored,, and their caregivers may have been unavailable to them from a physical or emotional standpoint. Once these kids grow up, they have a tendency to isolate rather than to turn toward others when distressed.[6] This tendency developed as a coping mechanism and is a protective measure. When upset or distressed, the child with a rejecting caregiver may have taken this message away from a circumstance they could not yet fully understand: "Well, I feel like total crap, but this person in my environment isn't helping, so I guess I'm on my own. To hell with asking other people for help, because when I do, they don't give it to me."

Or "Feeling rejected sucks nard, so one way to protect myself is to not speak up about anything."

Think about the implications your first attachments have on your life today. When you feel distressed or upset, do you turn toward the people who care about you, or away from them— either you shut down or turn to an unhealthy outlet, perhaps? Do you feel supported or defensive when someone asks how you are? It depends on the friend and on the tone they use, I know, but in general, do you see other people's concern as genuine or intrusive?

If you are inclined to reject the care that others have for you, you are perpetuating a kind of crappy pattern of interaction that you learned from your avoidant attachments. What do you think avoidance does to a romantic relationship—or a friendship, for that matter? Bring you closer?? Heck no, guys, it drives you apart!

Don't panic—there's a flip side.

If avoidance and shutting down are things you learned as a kiddo, you're pretty much a badass. As a clinical psychologist, I know you did what needed to be done in order to survive the environment you were put into. You had to be self-sufficient to get your needs met, because the person you relied on for help blew it and let you down hard. As a result, independence and self-reliance—and maybe isolation and defensiveness—became integral components of your coping strategies. It served you well because it helped you survive your environment when you were a kid, but now. . . it may be time to reevaluate those behaviors. They may not be doing you any good.

I don't want to sound like I am berating all parents here. I know it is difficult to raise a child, and I'm not assigning all the blame for everyone's unhappiness and suckiness to their parents. What I'm saying is that the actions and inactions of primary caregivers in the formative years of a child's life either support or delay healthy emotional development. That, my friends, is the stone-cold truth.

The good news is that you can change the attachments you form as the grown-ass person you now are. Unhealthy can become healthy and insecure can become secure. If you want emotional intimacy and to connect with others in a meaningful way, you have to challenge the negative ideas that got implanted into that beautiful head of yours when you were a young un.

You must take a risk and open yourself up to accept the love that someone else has for you. A part of you used avoidant or ambivalent behavior as a defensive tactic. It wasn't spawned out of evil by your psyche. It was created out of love to offer you protection from mental and emotional pain. Now, if you can thank that part of you, the part that came to your defense, for protecting you when you were younger, it might be easier for you to let go of it as an adult. You don't have to rely on those defenses to protect you anymore, because you're a grown-ass person with the ability to learn how to repair and heal from events that cause you pain. You can learn how to believe in yourself and handle life's shitstorms without falling to pieces (the rest of the book is going to help teach you this).

the actions and inactions of PRIMARY CAREGIVERS *in the formative* YEARS *of a child's life either* SUPPORT *or* DELAY *healthy emotional* DEVELOPMENT

Your magnificent psyche taught you to be self-reliant, and now, as an adult, it's okay for you to outgrow it and try something new. Your psyche wants you to be happy. Letting go of old strategies in exchange for new ones is a sign of strength and growth.

At birth, we are all sweet, perfect, beautiful babies with the potential for greatness. Nikola Tesla, Martin Luther King, Ingrid Newkirk, Jack White, and Marina Abramovic started out the same way as you and me. Now while we may very well start out as equals, at the same time we are also at the mercy of our caregivers to nurture our self-worth and instill in us a sense of security. Infusing a sense of security into that perfect, flawless, beautiful brain of yours is one of the most important jobs your primary caregiver will ever, ever, EvEr, EVER have. It's right up

WHEN YOU'RE An ADULT ACTING Consciously, YOU CREATE YOUR OWN Happiness, AnD you ARE in CHARGE of the RESULTS you See.

there with providing food, shelter, and clothing. So whether your caregiver was a sultan, genie, pirate ship captain, bakery owner, teacher, or factory worker, one of their jobs was to engender a secure bond with you.

Nothing trumps this, because it makes learning how to be a happy, emotionally healthy, loving, considerate, socially conscious adult (big picture here) possible. This does not mean that if you had any sort of insecure attachment to your caregiver you are doomed to a life of shit-misery, void of meaning and purpose. P'shaw! It just makes it trickier for you to get to that happy, meaningful place. Not impossible.

You can outgrow old strategies that your psyche created to protect you and keep you safe, because you are no longer at the mercy of your caregiver. You create your own destiny and you can begin to untangle the gnarly mess of your dysfunctional past.

When you're an adult acting in a conscious manner, you create your own happiness, and you are in charge of the results you see.

You need to understand your attachment bond with your primary caregiver and its influence throughout your life, to guide your little train out of the hideous mess someone else may have run it into—and onto the track you want.

You are powerless over the situation you are born into. Sometimes folks blame themselves and say, "I was a bad kid, and that's why my mom yelled at me so much."

I disagree. We each have a particular temperament and disposition, but it is not your fault if your caregiver was unavailable or unsupportive during your formative years. You can't blame yourself for what happened when you were younger. As an adult, it's a different story. It is a good thing to be accountable, but blaming yourself for something you had no control over will create misery.

Shit rolls downhill, and if you look around and realize you're on that turdball, now's your chance to jump off and release the guilt and shame you might be holding onto. I mean, the longer you stand on that dookie ball, the more you'll sink in, and you don't want that, so jump the heck off!

As you read on, know this: regardless of your upbringing and all your experiences to this point, you are precious and worthy of love and all the good things life has to offer. You have consciousness, free will, and the ability to make choices that will serve you better. You'll figure out how to do this if you stay with me, so keep on a'reading if you want to take charge of that marvelous life of yours!

Chapter 2 | Depression: How to stop feeling like a turd

Depression happens

Ever get that shit, dank feeling that life sucks, we suck, people suck and everything else sucks? The one where you feel hopeless, bummed, all-around sad, and can't see a good future? Whether it's the end of a relationship, a career that drains the life out of you, low self-esteem, the death of a loved one, postpartum blues, or feeling bummed about your life, financial situation, or future, the feelings I'm describing here are those of depression. Depression is one nasty little hussy/goober that sinks its claws into the best of us at times. Since it's a shared experience that can make a serious impact on those of us in the human race, getting rad necessitates we learn how to overcome it. By the end of this chapter, you should be able to understand what depression is, how you are playing a part in it, and what must happen if you want to get rid of it and change your emoji from ☹ to ☺.

What are you telling yourself?

When we experience something—an event, a situation, a conversation, or whatever—we infuse it with meaning. This process lights up activity centers in your brain and creates messages you then send to yourself.

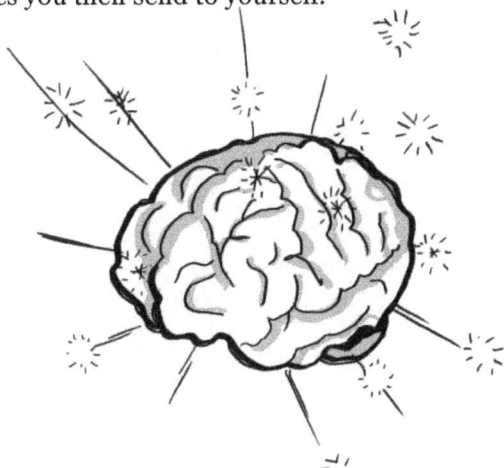

These are messages being created and delivered by you, to you, throughout your life.

One example of a message you may have sent yourself when you were younger is "Mom is nice. I can trust her." Or "Mom is a butt and she doesn't really have my back." A message you may be sending yourself as an adult or young adult with low-ish self-esteem may be "I don't look like Y, so I will never be happy," or "I haven't had the same opportunities as Z, so I can't amount to much," or "I'm not as Instagram popular as X; therefore I am less significant as a person."

These messages are significant because the more we repeat them, the more we believe them to be true. If your mom was a butt, maybe as an adult you then start to feel unworthy or undeserving of love. You may tell yourself that you deserve negative treatment from others because you are worthless. If you compare yourself to others and suffer from low self-esteem, you will continue to feel unhappy until you decide to accept yourself. If you haven't been as privileged as some other people, and you feel hopeless about being successful, you won't be motivated to try to achieve greatness.

The messages we give ourselves can be quite sinister. I mean, positive messages are great, ones that generate confidence, self-esteem, and feelings of worth, but the negative ones are tricky dastards because they can be subtle. Some people aren't even aware of the nasty messages they send to themselves until they try therapy and get someone like me on their side ,working to get those sneaks exposed.

Defining feelings and emotions

Although feelings and emotions are similar, and the terms are sometimes used interchangeably, the difference between them is that feelings incorporate what is experienced as a result of your five senses interacting with your environment. So, if we *touch* a hot stovetop, we feel pain, if we see a homeless couple with two children, we feel sadness, or if we *hear* a song we love, we feel joy.

Emotions, on the other hand, can be produced by a thought, memory, or external source, like a feeling. Emotions are not *necessarily* based on our senses. . . but they can be, and they're believed to be longer-lasting than feelings. So, when I come home from work and see my hilarious husband, I feel excited, but the emotion I have, which is long-lasting, is happiness.

Another reason it's tricky to tell them apart is that feelings and emotions can generate the same reaction sometimes. When I read a story about bullying, it makes me feel sad, and my emotion is also sadness (and anger, too). When I volunteer at my local clubhouse for developmentally disabled adults, I feel happy (I get to hang out with some of the coolest people on earth!) and my emotion is happy, too. So, there is overlap, but the two are separate entities.

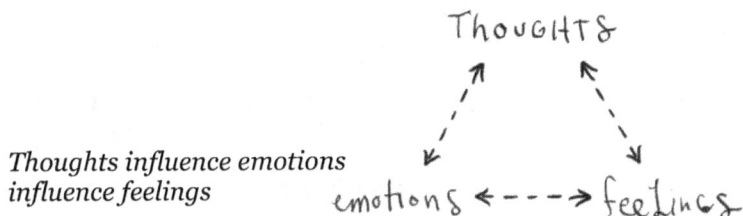

ThouGHTS

Thoughts influence emotions influence feelings

emotions ← - - → feelings

The lessons we learn and messages we take away from an experience influence our thoughts, our thoughts influence our emotions, and our emotions influence the way we feel (physically and mentally). This progression all works together, and it can be reversed: the way we feel influences our emotions, which influences our thoughts, which influence the messages we send ourselves. When we feel depressed, it sets off a chain reaction that affects all of these elements.

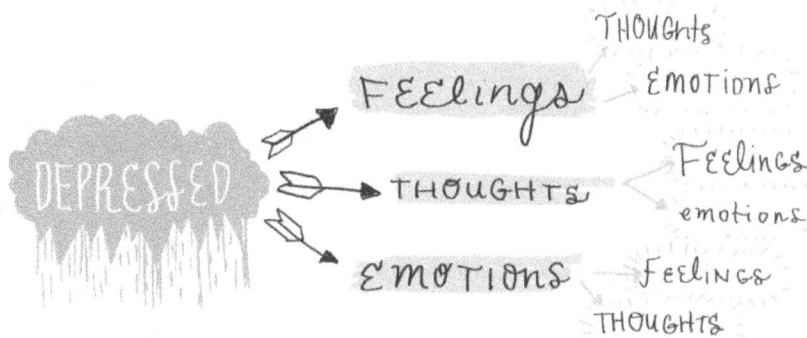

THOUGHts
FEElings → EmoTions
Feelings
DEPRESSED → THOUGHTS
emotions
EMOTIONS ← FEELINGS
THOUGHTS

What exactly is depression?

Depression is internalized sadness, and on some level internalized anger, plus the negative thoughts that accompany these emotions. In the most basic sense, it's anger and sadness wrapped tight together and drilling into your psyche so hard that they take away your hope, energy, and will, and distort your thinking. Depression takes a dump on your feelings then sets them on fire, and fucks with your head to the point that you start to think and believe things that are untrue. *No bueno.*

I include anger in my definition of depression, but this is sometimes hard for people to identify with. Focusing on the sadness part, because it is more noticeable, is natural, but I think that if you look hard enough they're both there. If someone you care about dies, you are sad, but you are also angry on some level. If you apply for a job and don't get an interview, you experience sadness on one hand and anger on the other. Same goes for asking someone out and getting rejected. You may be sad, but you're also angry. These are normal feelings, and I'm not saying that these situations automatically induce depression, or that feeling sad and angry about something yields depression, but the two often go together like bosom buddies. When you feel one, the other guy might be hiding in your state of mind, too.

The criteria to be formally diagnosed with depression hit on some of these:

- Feeling sad, empty, or irritable most of the day, almost every day, and/or being easily tearful
- Loss of interest in activities that once brought you joy and satisfaction
- Changes in weight (5% more or less than your usual weight in a month)
- Insomnia or hypersomnia, i.e., not being able to sleep or wanting tons of it
- Fatigue or loss of energy
- Slowed physical and emotional reactions; your thoughts and actions are delayed and you are way more sluggish than usual
- Feelings of guilt, worthlessness, and/or self-loathing
- Decreased ability to concentrate, increased indecisiveness
- Thoughts of death and suicide[1]

All your feelings ARE ALWAYS OKAY, all of the TIME

If you have thoughts of suicide, there is no doubt about it that you should seek immediate treatment, and if you currently feel that you might harm yourself, you need to go to the nearest emergency room. If you don't have suicidal thoughts but do have four or more of the nine symptoms listed above, and have felt this way for at least two weeks, you should seek professional help, and talk to a local psychologist, counselor, or licensed social worker.[2] Even if you have one symptom, if you can't seem to shake it and you continue to feel down, talking to someone could help. The two most common issues for which people seek help in clinics across the US are depression and anxiety, so trust me, if you feel depressed you're not alone. Asking for help is a sign of strength.

How can you stop feeling depressed?

The first step in eliminating depression is to accept that *all your feelings are always okay, all of the time.*

You have a right to feel the way you do. You are entitled to feel sad and dejected at times, just as you are entitled to feel happy and excited. I'm not trying to take your feelings away here, I'm just trying to help you ditch the ones that are bringing you down, so you can live a more happy and fulfilling life and dig out of the funky rut quicker than before.

For many of us, depression is a mood or emotional state that takes a certain amount of time to get through. The amount of time depends on the person and the issue they're dealing with. Different people's episodes, or bouts with depression, can last anywhere between a few hours, 1+ days, 1+ weeks, 1+ months, 1+ years, or even 1+ decades.

You gotta feel it to heal it

I often say, "Ya gotta feel it to heal it" and this applies to depression. You should allow yourself to feel your feelings, but this doesn't mean you have to get stuck there. After you have felt depressed for however long your process imposes, and are ready to trade in those doo-doo feelings for better ones, then you are ready to move out of the feeling part of your brain, and into the thinking part. Since our thoughts influence our feelings, one way to change our feelings is by working on changing our thoughts.

Get out of the feeling state and into the thinking state

Ask yourself "What am I doing to stay depressed?" The truth is, when we feel like dung *and can't seem to get over it,* there is something we're doing to perpetuate it. Research shows that something called cognitive appraisals show strong associations with symptoms of depression. A cognitive appraisal is a fancy-schmancy psych term, which means the way we interpret what happens to us, or the meaning we ascribe to situations we experience.

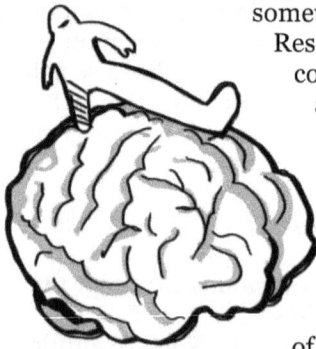

Cognitive appraisals, like some of the messages we send ourselves, can happen on a subconscious level, and we may not even be aware of the ways we are sabotaging our own happiness.

Example: I smiled at Bobby today at work, but he didn't smile back. A negative appraisal would be telling yourself, "Derp, I'm such a fundark. Why would Bobby ever give me the time of day?"

This negative appraisal is bunk. You don't know the real reason he didn't smile back, but you're assuming you do. The reality could have been that Bobby wasn't wearing his glasses today and he couldn't see you clearly. Poor guy didn't even know you smiled at him in the first place, but the way you spun the situation was negative and left you feeling bad about yourself.

Who or what made you feel bad? Your own thoughts and appraisal.

The good news is that *Although you're sometimes your own BIGGEST foe, you also hold the POWER to be your BEST ALLY.*

Expose negative thoughts

In his book *Change Your Brain, Change Your Life*, psychiatrist Daniel Amen identifies one of the biggest factors keeping you down: your very own Automatic Negative Thoughts, or ANTS.[3] ANTS are cynical, disturbing, upsetting, and dark thoughts that invade your brain, set up shop, and eventually invite all their friends: gloomy, snotty, saddy, dreary, teary, and meany. Feel free to add your own adjective here: _____y. Automatic negative thoughts stem from stink appraisals you make in situations where you are hypercritical or skew things in a negative direction.

Dr. Amen explains, "People who are depressed have one dispiriting thought following another. When they look at the past, they feel regret. When they look at the future, they see anxiety and pessimism. In the present moment they're bound to find something unsatisfactory. The lens through which they see themselves, others, and the world has a dim grayness."

People who are depressed see the world in a different way than those who are not. Unless one person has a vision impairment, in the physical sense both camps are viewing the same stimuli, but emotionally and psychologically... forget about it, the differences are supersized.

It's the difference between feeling a sense of awe upon watching a sunset and seeing it like Agnes Skinner of *The Simpsons* and commenting, "Thank God there's only one of those a day."

Our thoughts create our reality

Please, please, please repeat this and let it sink in:

YOUR THOUGHTS CREATE YOUR REALITY

Not literally speaking, that is; if you think, "I will wake up a billionaire, sleeping next to Tom Hardy," that doesn't mean that overnight he will teleport from his beautiful wife and into your bed. What this does mean, though, is that if you are depressed, pessimistic about your life, and hopeless about your future, then guess what? Your life will not change and your future will be sucky. It's a little thing called the self-fulfilling prophecy.

If you experience incessant depression, you don't expect good things to happen to you, and you won't try very hard to actualize them for yourself. Even if a good thing does come your way, you may not recognize it, or you will figure out a way to minimize it. Your motivation level is kaput and your desire to change and get better is deflated because you lack the energy you think it takes to get there.

If you are already convinced that the outcome will be horrible (or that going to therapy, or exercising, or talking to a friend, or eating better, or even just leaving the house, for example, won't do anything to help), you sabotage yourself and tighten the ties that bind you to your own personal cell of despair and misery.

I'm not chastising you here. I have empathy for you. Like millions of other people, I've been depressed, so I know that not being able to see a future for yourself is horrible. But if you're ever going to get out of that dank, dark place, you have to change the way you ingest and think about life. This is a must; there's no other way around it.

What's going on in my head when I feel like poop sprinkled with ball hair?

It's not all your fault. There are neurochemical processes going on in that head of yours, of which you are not even aware when you feel this way. The cells in your brain are constantly shooting back information to each other, which has an impact on your mood. I'll try to 101 the biology part of it here.

The deep limbic system

There is a walnut-sized part near the center of your brain that does a job of massive importance. The deep limbic system, or DLS, is where emotions are created, and it plays a major role in setting the emotional tone for your life.[4]

When your DLS is less active, you experience a general sense of hope and positivity. By contrast, the more riled up it is, the more negativity you feel. So if one of your parents was a jerk to you when you were a kiddo, or butthead kids picked on you a lot at school, you may have experienced the frequent activation of your DLS and you may be more accustomed to feeling bad now. You got used to having an overactive DLS, so now you feel bad out of habit.

So when people with a history of DLS activation get mad, sad, or stressed, their change from zero to a reactive state can be very quick. On the other hand, people with a history of infrequent DLS activation have more filters and self-control, because their DLS isn't used to getting so riled up. So those with infrequent activation of DLS are less likely to have a strong reaction, and more able to cope in healthy ways when anger, sadness or stress shows up on their radar.

If we have positive, consistent, and stable experiences, it is easier for our brains to process various experiences in positive ways, and our DLS does not become riled up. However, if we suffer from trauma, tragedy, pain, ridicule, and suffering, it's easier for our brains to process experiences in negative terms and over-activate the DLS. Just as the more you do something, the better you become, the more your DLS reacts a certain way, the better it becomes at continuing to react that way.

If you have a history of feeling down and out, chances are you're more inclined to activate that DLS of yours.

Over time, you've established these grooves and pathways in your brain, so that when something triggers you to feel sad, distressed, or angry, instead of being able to cope in the moment, maybe for you, your DLS is activated and you get worked up real fast.

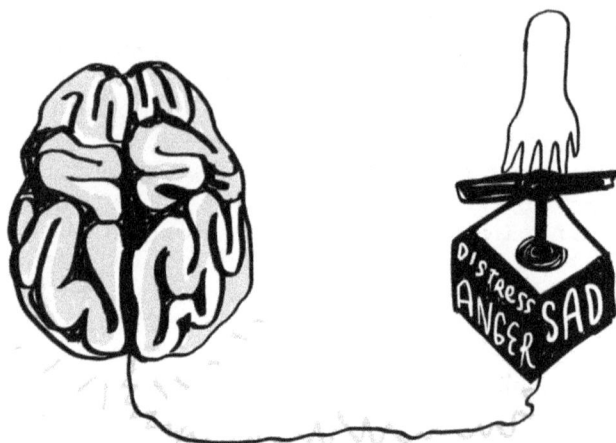

Women be trippin—important for guys to know, too

Females have been accused of being notoriously emotional and touchy, and in fact, research shows that women have larger deep limbic systems than men. This is both a good and a bad thing. Good, because it means that women (in general) are more in touch with their emotions, find it easier to express their feelings, and are better able to bond and connect with others.

Now, don't get me wrong, I love being a girl, because we're passionate, caring, and empathetic, but let's face it, we're also totally emo and sad-ballz sometimes. The flop side of having a larger DLS is that it makes females more vulnerable to developing depression. And yes, we are extra-susceptible during times of hormonal changes, including at the onset of puberty, before our periods (oh damn, I'm talking about PMS here), after the birth of a baby (postpartum depression is very real), and during menopause.

This is not to say that fellas don't get down, too. Of course they do; we all do sometimes.

It's NORMAL to EXPERIENCE DEPRESSION, BUT NOT SO NORMAL TO GET STUCK THERE.

And when you do, inside your head, what's happening is that your DLS is acting up and going haywire.

The prefrontal cortex vortex

Another reason the DLS is so darn important is that other parts of your brain, which serve essential functions are closely connected. One of the most crucial influences the DLS has is on the prefrontal cortex, a magnificent part of human biology that enables us to be goal-directed, driven, and effective. It lets us feel the variety of human emotion—from happiness, joy, and excitement, to sadness, grief, and despair. Additionally, this little gem gives us impulse control, a conscience, a sense of responsibility, and the ability to learn from our past.[5]

Are you or do you know someone who keeps repeating the same mistakes? Chances are, this person has an issue with their prefrontal cortex functioning . Rather than base their actions on previous experience, these folks invest most of their energies into fulfilling their immediate wants and needs. They lack self-awareness and are less able to make insightful choices when it comes to their behavior.

PLEASE PAY ATTENTION TO THIS: In addition to the above functions, the prefrontal cortex is also what helps a person insert rational thought into their emotional states. It helps people balance their emotions with logic and prevents negative emotions from overriding rationality. This is key when you are trying to cope with, get through, and get over depression, because it helps you step out of your feeling state of mind and into the thinking part. This will kickstart your heart and can get you out of drowning in the quicksand of depression.

Why it's so fucking hard to be fucking rational sometimes.

The main reason it is so hard for us to be rational when we feel emotional is pure biology: your reaction to experiences is emotional before your ability to be rational kicks in.

you experience things emotionally before your ability to be Rational Kicks in.

This is because your ability to reason is at the front of your brain, and the electrical signals that give birth to your feelings enter from the back of your brain.

Stay with me now. The meaning we inject into experience generates our feelings. The meaning we inject has to do with the way we interpret events. The way we interpret events has to do with how the sensory data gets filed. Everything we hear, see, touch, taste, and smell travels through our body in the form of electrical signals.

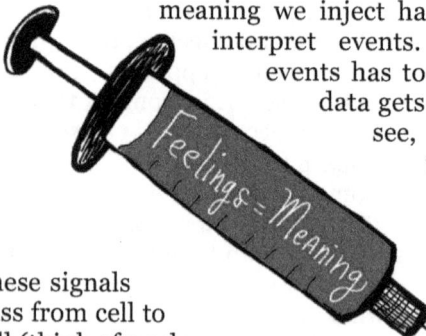

These signals pass from cell to cell (think of a relay race) until they reach the limbic system at the back of your brain.[6]

You may be thinking that sensory experience is cut and dried, as in, if you or I or the Queen of England smell a diaper on the beach, we cringe. Yes, that may be true, but there is variability in the way human beings interpret sensory information. For example, when I see a stranger smile at me, I think of it as a friendly gesture, but someone else may see that same stranger smile and assume they have ulterior motives or are laughing at them. We witnessed the same stimuli, but had different interpretations.

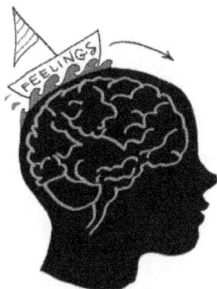

After feelings are triggered in the back of your brain, they encounter your midbrain, then move on to the frontal and prefrontal cortices, where rational thinking happens. We really do have a feeling part of our brains and a thinking part.

Screwed-up brain systems

Fight-or-flight erroneously triggered

Now, whether you're Christian, Hindu, Islamic, Buddhist, Jewish, agnostic, atheist, Wiccan, whatever, think about the evolutionary implications here. Historically, it would make sense that, for our survival, information first came in through the limbic system. Our ancestors encountered threats to their lives on a regular basis, and when they had to run the fuck away from a bear, do you think they had time to be rational? Not really. Our predecessors relied on their emotions to dictate their next moves. As in, an intense fear response (emotion) would trigger a person's fight-or-flight instinct, so they could take immediate action and tear ass outta wherever they needed to, in order to survive.

Here and now, in the 21st century, though. . . our internal system for threat detection can get jacked up because we perceive things that are not really that threatening as threats. Perhaps you get a bad review from your boss at work, or your husband doesn't compliment your new hairdo, or only four of your friends like your Facebook status update; these things are appropriate grounds for an emotional reaction, but if you can't let it go and can't get out of your emotional brain (DLS) and into your rational/thinking part (frontal cortex), you're in for trouble. Not being able to get out of the emotional part of your brain makes you vulnerable to depression.

Depression and the DLS

Here is a checklist for factors that suggest you have some problems with your DLS, making you more susceptible to depression:

- feelings of irritability
- moodiness
- low motivation
- a tendency to socially isolate
- a propensity to spin events negatively
- overwhelming negative feelings, including hopelessness and sadness
- appetite and sleep problems[7]

Depression and the prefrontal cortex

Here is a checklist for factors that suggest problems with your prefrontal cortex, the center of your ability to be rational:

- emotional bluntness or disconnection
- poor judgment
- difficulty being moral
- misperceptions of others and environmental cues
- disorganization
- short-term memory issues
- poor time management
- lack of perseverance
- impulse-control problems
- inability to learn from the past
- inability to form insight
- hyperactivity and/or distractibility[8]

Can you see the overlap between problems with being able to manage your feelings and problems with being rational? A lack of motivation negatively affects perseverance. Excess irritability may prevent you from having insightful thoughts. And a person who feels moody may misperceive the intentions of others.

How thinking affects feelings

Misunderstandings make you unhappy

Can you think of any times that you misperceived the intentions of someone else, or when someone else misperceived yours? C'mon, just name one. I'll even give you a personal example, because we're all adults here and I'm a work in progress, too.

Like a lot of women, sometimes I am extra-emotional and hypersensitive to the treatment I receive from my husband, more-so when I'm holding pennies (i.e., menstruating). So, if we're hanging out and he goes to get a drink for himself and doesn't ask if I want anything, or if he zones out on his phone texting instead of talking to me during dinner, I become sad and say something like this to myself: "Man, what happened to us? If this was the first year we were dating, you would have been bending over backwards to be nice, and now you don't even consider that I may be thirsty too, or even care to have a conversation with me. What a bummer. This is so shitty. I feel despair and I'm now getting depressed about what our future looks like."

Enter awareness. If I become aware of some of the irrationality going on with my thinking, then I am better able to stop myself when I have these thoughts that breed depression. By inserting rationality into my view, I can remind myself that not being asked if I want something to drink does not mean my husband hates me and only cares about himself. Maybe he had something important on his mind. I can remember that as a thirty-three-year-old adult, I can use my big girl voice to communicate to him that it hurts my feelings when he doesn't want to talk to me during dinner (and realize that I do that same thing sometimes too :/). Instead of just sulking in my shit depressive state, I can try to resolve it.

Pulling yourself out of mega-sad, annoyed, pissed mode incorporates mindfulness, which means bringing your attention to the present experience and holding it there as the experience occurs. (We will address mindfulness in greater detail later.)

Managing your mindset can make you happy

Rationality = Relief

If you are able to insert rationality into your awareness, then you can de-escalate your intense emotional state, stop a bad mood from inflating into depression, and begin

to cure your depression, if it's already escalated to that. By "inserting rationality," I mean using reasoning and reality-based thinking to help you take your feelings down a couple of notches. Remember, I don't want to take your feelings away, I just want to help you learn how to manage them better. Once you can manage them better, you are able to gain control over your emotional state and all its glorious intensity. If you are successful at doing this, what's happening in physical terms behind the scenes inside your head, is that you are allowing your emotions to move into your prefrontal cortex, so that reasoning and rational thought processes can take place. **In essence you're hopping from the fiery reaction part into the soothing, rational part.** This trains your DLS to be less reactive in the future, too.

Have you ever talked yourself out of a bad mood or used rational thinking to lower the intensity of

your feelings about something when they were incredibly strong? If so, that's proof you can change your thinking and deactivate your DLS, so that your prefrontal cortex functions more smoothly.

Not to say you shouldn't be passionate about things. This is more in reference to the times when you thought someone couldn't care less if you were dead because they didn't ask if you wanted anything from the kitchen when they got up. Or when that lady cut in front of you at the U-Scan and you felt utterly victimized, or when someone gave your best friend a dirty look and you tasted blood. Those are the times we need 1,000 ccs of rationality, stat.

Conclusion

At some point in your life, it's probable that you will feel depressed. If and when this happens, it's okay, natural, normal, and something that you need to accept. But if you get depressed and can't get out of it, that's not so okay, natural, or normal, because it will start to lower your quality of life. Maybe you're prone to depression because of your past or out of habit, and now your DLS gets easily activated. Maybe not. Causes vary, but your manner of thinking is a contributing factor. If you're able to expose your negative thinking, debunk some of those bunk views, and see how your thoughts have a direct impact on your mood, it will be easier to recover.

Your thoughts create your reality, so learning to respond to your feelings with rationality will help you overcome a depressive mood at a faster rate. Yes, ya gotta feel it to heal it, so don't try to deny depression. But also, don't allow yourself to stall out in that shit-garbage misery town. It's okay to visit, just don't settle down there. If you can't do this on your own, seeking professional help from a licensed psychologist or social worker is a good idea. Understanding these ideas and applying them to your life will help stop your suffering.

Chapter 3 | You can change your thoughts and fix your brain

A big chunk of what my fellow psychologists and I do, is to help people learn how to change the way they think. That is to say, we help them see the bogus views they have, then give them the tools they need to trade em in for more positive, realistic ones. Sometimes this takes two months, sometimes two years, sometimes twenty+ years, depending on the person and their history.

To begin to combat depression, I'm going to give you some tricks of the trade. These are found in some of the really popular techniques of psychotherapy, and they might sound all scientific'ey, but bear with me, because they're important.

Cognitive behavioral therapy is one of the most common interventions practiced by mental health clinicians. This treatment is designed to help people identify the dysfunctional and distorted views of reality they hold. The idea is that once these views are illuminated and brought into an individual's awareness, he or she can learn how to defeat, refute, and disprove them.[1]

This technique teaches people how to

1. monitor negative, automatic thoughts
2. recognize how thoughts, feelings, and behaviors are interrelated
3. find evidence that supports dysfunctional and distorted thinking, then scrutinize it
4. substitute reality-based thoughts for irrational ones
5. identify and change dysfunctional beliefs that lead to distorted views

Certain kinds of thoughts keep you depressed

Dysfunctional, distorted, and coo coo inaccurate thoughts—which you might not even realize you have—reinforce feelings of depression. These inaccurate thoughts are important to identify because they are a big part of what's keeping you depressed.

Once you shed light on them, it'll be easier to gain control and melt them away. You can't fight a monster if you don't know where it is, so bringing these thoughts into your awareness will give you the upper hand to fight em off.

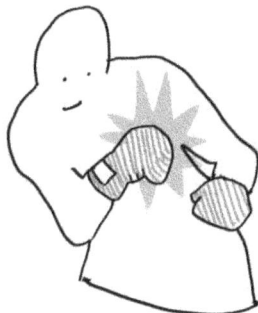

Dysfunctional and distorted beliefs

Here is a list of ten common cognitive distortions that people make—and lucky for you, a B*O*N*U*S distortion, because human beings are just that neurotic (present company included), bringing our grand total to eleven.[2] These dysfunctional views contribute to depression, so as you review them, pay attention to the ones you commit. Ain't nobody watching and ain't no shame in it; we all do this stuff sometimes, and calling yourself out leads to growth. You need to be honest with yourself if you're ever going to make a change for the better, by exposing dysfunction and defeating the inaccurate beliefs that are making you feel like a fart face.

1.) All-or-nothing thinking

All-or-nothing thinking is seeing things in categories of black and white and leaving no room for gray area.

For example, if you break up with your girlfriend or boyfriend, you might say to yourself, "It's all my fault, I am such a stupid idiot, I'll never meet anyone else again because I am so damaged."

This, my friend, is a stone-cold fallacy, not based in reality, and it produces inaccurate thoughts. It's not usually all one person's fault when a relationship ends.

2.) Overgeneralization

Overgeneralization is seeing a single negative event as a never-ending pattern of defeat.

Say you have been trying to lose weight, and you're doing well, but it's happening much slower than you want. The moment you gain one pound, out of ten lost, you might say to yourself, "I have to work so hard and it doesn't even matter. Weight loss comes so easy for so many other people. I am destined to be a big fat pig. FML." Again, not true, and telling yourself this perpetuates inaccurate thoughts that may lead you to give up before you reach your goal.

3.)Mental filter

Operating with a mental filter is picking out a single negative detail and dwelling on it until your reality becomes gloomy. Think of a drop of ink that mixes into a gallon of water and colors it all gray.

Say you're having a great day, are in a good mood, and just left the flower shop with a gorgeous bouquet of poppies for your wife. . . when you notice a scratch on your car. Yes, this blows, and you don't know who did it, but if you let it ruin your whole night because you are hyperfocused on it and can't let it go, then you're committing the mental filter distortion here.

4.) Disqualifying the positive

Disqualifying the positive is rejecting praise by insisting for some reason that it's irrelevant or doesn't count.

For example, say you're an artist who completed a series of paintings. If you renounce the positive feedback you receive from others, it will be impossible for you to experience the good feelings they're dishing out. Instead of taking in all that goodness, you deny yourself a positive experience. This is dysfunctional because it contributes to low self-worth and low self-esteem.

5.) Jumping to conclusions

Jumping to conclusions is skewing things in a negative direction and making biased interpretations, even though there is no evidence to support your conclusion. There are two major forms of this.

- Mind-Reading: Arbitrarily concluding that someone is responding negatively to you, but not bothering to verify your hypothesis.

- **The Fortune-Teller Error**: Anticipating that things will turn out bad and feeling convinced that your prediction is fact and cannot be altered.

An example of mind-reading: Say you are walking, and you look up, only to make eye contact with a person you find attractive. Their expression is totally neutral, and all you have to go on is the one second of eye contact you shared. If you determine that the other person was judging you, your view of reality is distorted. The spin you put on it reflects your negative beliefs about yourself and your defensiveness.

The fortune-teller error is an unusually tricky one, but quite common in a lot of us. For example, in my office I'll often hear ". . . because, Tiffany, I knew it wouldn't do any good," or "I knew it wouldn't make a difference." Really. So that's why you blew off your job interview? Or why you didn't talk to your friend about how his pot-smoking is out of control, or why you didn't ask the girl that you like to hang out? How do you know it would have gone the way you think? The only way to have known, is to have actually checked it out and gained that experience. Would you know what bull testicles taste like without ever taking a bite? Nah, you wouldn't. You need the experience to know. Yes, history is a good predictor sometimes, but it's not always consistent.

6.) Magnification or minimization

Magnifying is exaggerating the importance of events; minimizing is downplaying them until they appear insignificant.

An example of magnification: A female friend you find attractive gives you a hug, and you think she is hitting on you and probably fantasizes about the two of you rockin the casbah and doing sex to each other. If you do this, you're taking a single gesture and blowing it way out of proportion. As in turning a little seahorse into an orca.

Another common way we commit magnification is through Facebook, Instagram, and Twitter. Social media is supposed to be fun, but some people hate it because it makes them feel like hippo shit. Yes, other people have good stuff going on in their life, but if they share it, and you see it and it makes you feel like wet donkey balls, then it is possible that you are magnifying their accolades.

Remember in the beginning when I said not to put people on pedestals? When you're stuck in magnification, you could be doing just that. And I guarantee that the person you magnify has stinky-assed flatus just like the rest of us.

An example of minimization: If your buddy drove home drunk for the third time this week and you pretended there wasn't anything wrong with that. As in, you minimize seriousness of this type of behavior and deny the fact that this could be a sign of alcoholism. You might minimize it by saying, "Oh that's just Sam being Sam." Or "He's having a rough month. He'll stop getting hammered once things with his girl get worked out." Not cool to do this, guys. It's like pretending a grizzly bear is a teddy bear. Or that a serving size is ten handfuls instead of one.

7.) Emotional reasoning

When you use emotional reasoning, you think your negative emotions are a reflection of the way things are in actuality. This happens when you believe your feelings without ever questioning them. Thinking with your feelings is imprecise, because sometimes your feelings are off base. (Remember, we feel things before we can be rational.)

Examples of emotional reasoning: You feel guilty, then reach the automatic conclusion that you must have done something ghastly. Or say you try something different with your hair, then your shit boss makes a snide comment about it that makes you feel bad. If you conclude—based on this single shitty comment from a woman who is miserable—that stepping outside the box and trying something different with your appearance will yield negative reactions, then you're committing this distortion.

Yes, your feelings have a right to be there, but sometimes they get coked out and trick you into believing a false reality, which perpetuates inaccurate thoughts and can lead to depression.

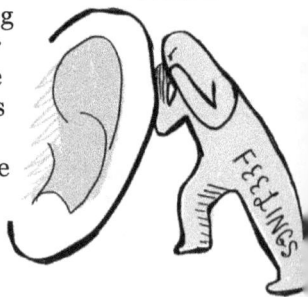

8.) "Should" statements

If you try to motivate yourself with "shoulds" and "shouldn'ts," it could mean you think you must punish and degrade yourself before you take action.

For example, if you try to shame yourself into action by telling yourself, "I should hit the gym because I'm a fat fatty ugly, stupid bitch. No one will ever want to be with me if I don't change, because I'm a worthless whale and if I don't do something about my appearance, I may as well pack mah bags and go live under the sea with all the other urchins."

OUCH! This kind of thinking is coo coo inaccurate and creates a risk that you will develop depression and other maladies, like low self-esteem and feelings of worthlessness.

9.) Labeling and mislabeling

Labeling and mislabeling is an extreme form of overgeneralization (distorted belief #2).

For example, say you're planning a party and head to the store to get supplies. If you forgot one of the thirty-three items on your list and end up feeling like a stupid sack of butt hair because of it, then you're labeling yourself as worthless and incompetent, even though there's no evidence to suggest that's true.

Being hypercritical of others is another form of this distorted thinking. Say someone you know tells a bad joke or pronounces a word wrong during a discussion you are having. If you pass harsh judgement and view them as being an ignorant douchebag, it's a sign that you are mislabeling them. It's a distortion to draw such extreme conclusions based on one piece of evidence, and when you do, you're the one being judgmental and condemnatory.

10.) Personalization

Personalizing is when you see yourself as the cause of an external negative event for which you were not responsible.

If you think your friend got her haircut because of you, or started listening to a certain kind of music because of you, you could be adopting this irrational view. An extreme example would be a victim of abuse blaming themselves for it because they believe they deserved it, or were "asking for it." Believing you are responsible for something that you are not connected to, and are actually independent of, can lead to trouble.

11.) Blaming

Blaming is when you fault someone or something for the problems in your life.

An example would be someone who is bitter because she never went to college, and blames her parents for not "forcing" her to go. Or someone who thinks it's his girlfriend's fault that he drinks, because it's the only way he can deal with the stress of the relationship. Or someone who thinks fast-food restaurants are responsible for making him fat.

There may be contributing factors as to why your life is the way it is, but putting too much emphasis on them tricks you into thinking you are not accountable. This is super horrible because when you evade responsibility by displacing it onto others (parents, partner, or friends), or onto your environment (fast food), you become a passive victim of circumstance, which makes it difficult for you to rise up and do a damn thing about it.

ya feel me?!

*R*E*V*I*E*W*
of distorted and dysfunctional thinking

- All-or-nothing thinking
- Overgeneralization
- Mental filter
- Disqualifying the positive
- Jumping to conclusions
- Mind-reading
- Fortune-teller error
- Magnification or minimization
- Emotional reasoning
- "Should" statements
- Labeling and mislabeling
- Personalization
- Blaming

How to be happy

Use your sweet, sweet consciousness to rid yourself of stinkin thinkin

Controlling your consciousness determines your quality of life. When you are able to insert rational thinking into your views, you are gaining essential control of your consciousness. Letting go of the thoughts keeping you shackled to misery enables you to take charge of the things you can control and increases your level of tolerance and acceptance for the things you can't.

you CAN CONTROL How YOU AllOW your ENVIRONMENT to AFFECT you.

You can control how you allow your environment to affect you. What you can't always control are the factors in that environment, including other people's behaviors and comments.

Trade irrational thoughts for rational ones

I often give my clients campy little sayings to chomp on in hopes of inciting insight, and one of these is "Ya gotta quit that stinkin thinkin." This is what you need to do if you are ever going to learn how to refute inaccurate beliefs that keep you down and cause misery, depression, and despair. The way to do this is to identify your irrational beliefs—and then disprove them.

What evidence do you have for any of the eleven distorted beliefs you hold? I may not know you, but I'm 100% sure that the evidence you have is faulty. Let's look at some common irrational thoughts (IT) and the rational statements (RS) that refute them.

IT: Everyone else has it easier than I do. Why do bad things always happen to me?
RS: Life is not always easy and I am not the only one who suffers. Somewhere in the world right now, there is another person who has more problems than I do. Just because I think other people have it super easy doesn't mean it's true.

IT: I'll never meet anyone and I'll die alone, decrepit, and miserable.
RS: I really want to meet someone to spend the rest of my life with, and it sucks being the only one of my friends without a mate. It's good to have standards, and not settling means I have self-esteem and love myself. I will remain hopeful, keep putting myself out there, and work on my own personal growth in the meantime.

IT: I will always be fat.
RS: My body's frame is due in part to genetics. If I want to lose weight there are options for me. I can be more mindful of what I'm eating and make an effort to exercise more if I want to see results. Also, a number on a scale does not determine self worth.

IT: I'm stuck at this shitty job in this shitty town until the day I die.
RS: I have free will and I am responsible for the choices I make. Student loans are available for me if I want to go to college, and I can save my money and move away if I want to.

IT: I should be a better person and do more for my family, friends, coworkers, and neighbors.
RS: I do the best that I can, and I deserve to spend my free time the way I want to. If helping these people will improve my well-being, I will do it, but on my own terms and in my own time. Saying no to people does not mean I am selfish.

Being happy is easy if you interpret your life in a positive way

According to Mihaly Csikszentmihalyi, a badass dude who has devoted over twenty-five years of his life studying happiness, happiness begins with gaining control over the contents of your consciousness.3 If and when you do this, you are learning and thereby pruning your brain for positive change. The more you do it—you guessed it—the easier it gets.

Csikszentmihalyi questions whether we're unhappy because mankind is destined to remain unfulfilled, or because we are seeking happiness in the wrong places, only to find chronic disappointment that can poison our outlook. After a quarter century of research, he has found that the latter is true, stating:

"... happiness is not something that happens. It is not the result of good fortune or random chance. It is not something that money can buy or power command. It does not depend on outside events, but rather, on how we interpret them."4

Do you guys understand what this means? It means that billionaires, movie stars, athletes and musicians have no more of an advantage for achieving happiness than any of the rest of us. So the guy porking Miss Universe and the guy porking Miss County Fair have the same opportunity to experience happiness. The kicker is in how you interpret your experiences.

THE MEANING you ascribe TO YOUR **LIFE, RELATIONSHIPS, FAMILY,** FRIENDS, CAREER AND EVERYTHING ELSE IS PRECISELY WHAT DETERMINES your Level of **HAPPINESS**

Understand that true happiness comes from within

A man in his thirties once told me that the point in life is to make "guys want to be you and girls want to fuck you." If you agree with this statement, you might have a hard time ever finding happiness. I'm a huge fan of the saying "different strokes for different folks," and I definitely don't believe that everyone's idea of happiness looks the same, but I do know that to base your level of happiness on an outside source will leave you empty and unfulfilled. If you extract validation and meaning solely from external sources (being admired by others, having as many status symbols as possible, valuing the superficial), your identity will be erased and you may transform into a hollow shell of a human.

Now don't get me wrong here; having money and being admired are not bad things. In fact, it often takes a great deal of talent to achieve them (I mean, look at the Kardashians, right?), so I'm not denouncing rich and famous people. I'm making the simple statement that they have the same abilities and capacities as the rest of us when it comes to achieving happiness. Yes, more money could make your life a bit easier, but it is not a fundamental cure for unhappiness. If it was, there would be no celebrity rehab, right?!

There is a huge difference between people who depend on external acknowledgment to determine their self-worth and those that do not. It's important to acknowledge this, because becoming independent of your social environment can alleviate depression. If you can find purpose and enjoyment regardless of your circumstances, you are better equipped to overpower depression when it busts into your life unwelcomed.

Changing to an internally motivated system takes work and requires you to stop putting so much weight on the rewards and punishments you get from external stimuli. Yes, supermodels are beautiful, but if you're hyperfocused on looking like one and weighing ninety-nine pounds, you are not on the road to happiness. If you're leasing a Mercedes and can't afford to sign your daughter up for ballet, you're not on the road to happiness. If you follow someone on Instagram because you think they are way better looking than you, have a superior life, and are more worthy a person than you are, you're not on the road to happiness. (If you follow them because you are a fan of theirs and believe they are a good person, that's different, because you are not judging yourself or placing them on a pedestal.)

Consciousness: Use it or lose it

Consciousness, or your state of awareness, is very powerful. So powerful that you can make yourself happy or miserable based on what you allow into it. Gaining control over your consciousness may require a drastic change in your attitude regarding what's important and what's not. The information we allow into our consciousness is of extreme importance because it is, in fact, what determines our quality of life.[5]

If you want to change the way you feel, Then you have to change the way you think.

If your consciousness is a canvas and you're the painter, your thoughts are the colors on your palette and you have some important decisions to make. You're going to paint a dark picture if you're working with thoughts like "I suck," "I'm a loser," or "I am broken and damaged." If you're working with thoughts like "I'm not where I want to be, but I can take steps to change this," "Everyone struggles with insecurities, and I can pick myself up," and "I am just as worthy as anyone else, and deserve to be happy too," you'll end up with a different painting.

REPEAT OUT LOUD: WE HAVE CONTROL OVER the WAY WE EXPERIENCE LIFE

Conclusion

We are not powerless against life. We are agents of change in our own lives because we have consciousness. Your consciousness can be your best friend or your biggest foe, and if you're not BFFs with yours already, I suggest you stop flooding it with distorted thoughts and start learning how to embrace the power of your mind. You can take the power back, start feeling confident, and unleash your awesomeness.

Depression is a twisted combination of feelings and thoughts that drill into your life and take a grave toll on your mood, energy level, and overall outlook. It's made up of feelings of sadness, hopelessness, misery, despair, and anger, and fed by distorted thoughts that reinforce them. Experiencing depression is normal, but staying depressed for more than two weeks is not, and if you feel this way and can't get out of it, getting professional help is a viable option.

In order to get out of your shit-feeling depressive state, you must learn to insert rationality into your view. This is a challenge, because we experience feelings before our thoughts kick in, and it's not uncommon to get stuck in our emotional brains. But identifying and disproving the distorted beliefs you hold is the key to getting out of your depressive state sooner.

You are in charge of the content you allow into your consciousness, and you can control the reactions you have to just about anything and anyone. You determine what is important in your life, and you are in charge of where you invest your energy and focus. That will influence the level of happiness you are able to experience. If you show excessive concern with external factors, including others' approval or points of view, you can lose sight of what's important and become more susceptible to depression and low self-esteem.

I promise: You have the power to set all of these beautiful things in motion for yourself, and you can do it if you learn how to make your feeling brain and your thinking brain dance, instead of playing tug-of-war.

Chapter 4 | Anxiety: If I don't piss myself,
I might just learn something

It's easy to get carried away with our thoughts, in particular when they have so much fear and anxiety in them. I try not to catastrophize too much, but like others, I am flawed and my anxiety can Tokyo Drift, going from 0–1,000,000 in 10 seconds without me even realizing it.

Here's what it sounds like in my head:

What if I write this book and everyone hates it? What if my husband and I get into a huge fight and we break up? What if my mom has cancer? What if I have cancer?! What if my minpins somehow get out of the house and get hit by a car, and then I come home and see their tiny guts and body parts scattered in front of the yard, and then my husband and I split, and my doctor calls to tell me that my mom and I both have cancer, and then I get 1,000 pieces of hate mail that say no one likes me, and then the house gets hit by lightning and starts on fire, and then the devil comes to drag me to hell and now I have to watch Barney reruns with Hitler for all of eternity? What if. . .

Yikes, not a good way to think. The good news is, there's hope. If you can feel compassion and can comprehend the fundamental nature of acceptance, you'll be able to deal with your anxiety in healthier ways. If you feel like a donkey's butt when those Sarah McLachlan ASPCA commercials come on (that's compassion), and if you can recognize that there are some things you have no power over, like the fact that you don't have liquid gold running through your veins (that's acceptance), then you can successfully manage your anxiety.

COMPASSION + ACCEPTANCE = ANXIETY RELIEF

How does this sound? Too good to be true? Well, it ain't. I know I've encouraged you to **give your emotions a hug and high five** instead of trying to punch them in the eye, stab them in the neck, or shank them in the back, and guess what? There is a whole science that supports doing this when it comes to anxiety. This is called acceptance and commitment therapy, or ACT.[1]

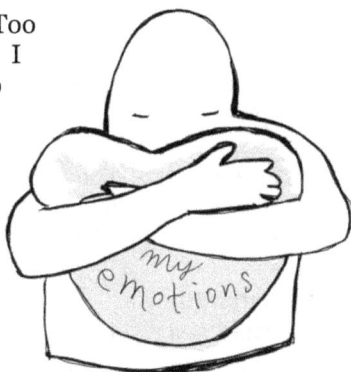

ACT is an approach to dealing with anxiety that says all we need to do is accept our thoughts and feelings—including the unwanted ones, because they need the most lovin—while moving toward our goals.

What the what?! That's it? That's all you have to focus on?

You're damn right, character, so get your butt in this truth booth and keep a readin. I'm bringing you the gold here—all you gotta do is pick it up.

What is anxiety, and how is it different from fear?

Anxiety is an emotion or mood state that makes you feel worried about the future. It is a normal human emotion that we all experience to varying degrees at times, because we do, in fact, think about the future. This little bugger (like any other emotion, when you think about it) has the potential to go super berserk. In order to improve the way you cope with anxiety, you must first have a deeper understanding of the nature of fear and worry in general.

Before we go on, it's important to note that although fear and anxiety often go hand in hand, they are two distinct phenomena and emotions.

Anxiety

Anxiety is a future-oriented mood state that brings with it worry and apprehension.[2] The sciency part is that anxiety activates our sympathetic nervous system, which is part of our autonomic nervous system. This is relevant because our autonomic nervous system is what triggers our fight-or-flight response. When we experience a future-based worry such as, "I hope my SUV doesn't spin out while I'm driving in this horrible Detroit snowstorm," we are nervous, scared, or terrified of what may happen. Constant anxiety about events that may happen in the near or distant future keeps our sympathetic nervous system in a heightened state of activity.

Here are some of the wonderful side effects of an excited sympathetic nervous system:

- panic attacks
- rapid heart rate
- poor sleep
- hypertension
- high cholesterol
- heart disease
- type 1 diabetes
- clotting diseases and stroke[3]

Not to mention all the other psychological distress, frustration, tension, and discomfort that goes along with it.

Fear

Fear, on the other hand, is a present-oriented mood state that occurs in response to a real or imagined threat.[4] So for those of us who live on the East Coast, fear would kick in the moment we actually hit that godforsaken ice patch on a snowy day and start spinning on the freeway (West Coast, substitute earthquakes and experiencing the ground move beneath your feet).

FEAR OPERATES IN REAL TIME, WHEREAS ANXIETY is based on something that may happen **IN THE FUTURE.**

Another difference between fear and anxiety is that fear involves behavioral actions, such as freezing, running, or escaping, versus anxiety, which involves verbal and cognitive actions, such as thinking and worrying or ruminating.

Fear, like anxiety, activates our sympathetic nervous system, but instead of keeping it in a heightened state, sends a surge of energy (think Frankenstein getting hit by lightning, 1931) that activates our fight-or-flight response and prepares us to bust a move.

It's important to note that while there are differences between anxiety and fear, the "DANGER! DANGER! Get the fuck out of here!" response is triggered when you feel either one. And either one can take a physiological toll on you, like increasing your heart rate and making you feel a tightness in your chest.

Fear and anxiety are perfectly normal

How they saved your caveman ass

One of the best things you can do to improve your ability to cope with fear and anxiety is to accept them as normal. The reality is that anxiety follows you, sometimes more often than you'd like. **It knocks on your door, tries to get your attention, and wants you to come hang out with it.** And there is a good reason for this—it goes way back to the times when our ancestors were kicking it on this earth, primal style.

Ask yourself: What has enabled our successful evolution? The answer is our survival skills. If you can think in terms of evolutionary significance, you can understand the utility of anxiety and fear.

If the experience of anxiety and fear is

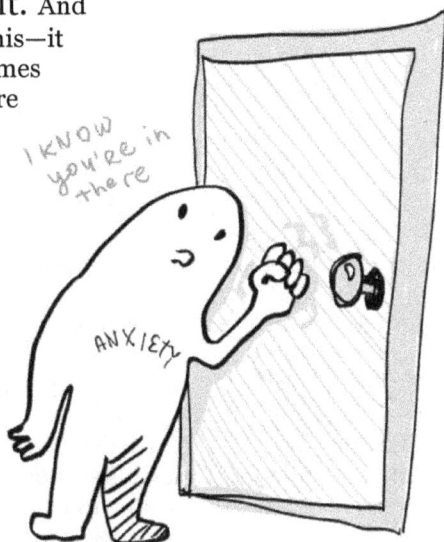

part of evolution, it means the experience is healthy, normal, and adaptive. It's the part where it goes nutzo that isn't so healthy, normal, and adaptive. Back in the *Jungle Book* days when our ancestors were grunting, starting fires, hunting, gathering, and getting buck-nasty to further our species, do you know what their main objective was every single day? It was DON'T DIE. The anxiety and fear responses they developed enabled them to escape danger and evade death. Since we evolved from badass mofos who literally ran away from tigers and lions, fought bears and wrestled wild animals with their bare hands in order to preserve their own lives, these responses are hardwired into our brains.

In this sense, anxiety and fear are natural alarms, which tell us to take protective action because our health, safety, and well-being are in danger. This is not a bad thing. Back in the day, the dudes without a fear response were probably the ones who walked off cliffs and ate their own poop.

The efficacy of this threat-activation system hinges on a "better safe than sorry" attitude.[5] We have been groomed to overestimate danger, which is sometimes good for survival, but often bad for our attention and focus.

Picture yourself as a Paleolithic hunter going past a cave back in the day. When you hear a noise, all your attention hyperfocuses on your surroundings and your body has a physiological response. This is a good thing. If you're going to make it past that cave alive, you have to invest all your energy and focus in scanning your surroundings and getting ready to shag ass as fast as you can. This natural alarm system was activated by fear and anxiety and it helped keep you alive.

How they save your modern ass

What initiates a fear and anxiety response now will sometimes be different than what initiated it for our ancestors. Take Tom, who had the hardest time letting go of the fact that his girlfriend told him she hates how he acts around his college friends. She said he drank too much, acted ignorant, and was misogynistic when they were around. She adored him the rest of the time, and she didn't understand why he changed so much in their presence. He couldn't let go of her using the word "hate" and kept focusing on it, saying stuff like, "She must secretly hate me deep down," and "I know she's planning on leaving me. I mean, she hates me, she even told me so."

In time, he was able to realize that she did a good thing by being honest with him, because she was venting her feelings instead of letting them fester until they built into a huge toxic ball of resentment that exploded everywhere. He also realized that he'd focused on the word "hate" because of the insecurity that it stirred up in him; it made him think he wasn't good enough. Upon further exploration, these insecurities revealed his fears and anxiety.

He came to see that he was afraid of losing her because he loved her. He even admitted that he acted like a knucklehead around these guys and was not always himself. Once he understood why the word "hate" had such a strong impact on him and how it was connected to his fear and anxiety, he ascribed meaning to the whole experience and it was easier for him to manage his feelings and get through the issue with his girlfriend.

How you learned to be anxious

Classical conditioning: learning by association

Research has shown that our threat-response system is not only activated by perceived threats, but also by things we associate with perceived threats. This is called learning by association, or classical conditioning. Just as Pavlov's pup made an association to the bell that rang at feeding time, humans make associations among stimuli in our environments, too, and this can lead to the development of anxiety.

Say, for example, you were exposed to parents who argued, or you had a hypercritical adult figure in your life, or you were picked on in school. As an adult, you may experience anxiety when you hear people arguing, when presented with an intellectual or physical challenge, or when you are in a large group. You learned to associate feelings of anxiety with those environments and experiences.

When an association is made between anxiety and another feeling—anger, stress, or embarrassment, for example—it creates a smorgasbord of triggers. When you have a feeling of anxiety, you also feel anger, stress, or embarrassment; then the feelings of anger, stress, or embarrassment lead you to feel anxiety. Since anxiety isn't a very pleasant feeling, you can see why folks would develop aversions to the emotions they associate with it.

Operant conditioning: learning through consequences

The second way we learn to be anxious is through consequences, which is called operant conditioning. This means that whether or not we repeat a behavior depends upon whether it brings about rewards or consequences. If we experience a reward after we behave a certain way, we are inclined to repeat that behavior. If we experience a consequence and have an adverse feeling, then we are less inclined to behave that way again.

What are some of the rewards you get from your behaviors? Do you feel happy when you are able to make someone laugh? Does it warm your heart when you help someone in need? Do you feel validated when you do something nice for someone you care about?

What about consequences? What are some behaviors that have caused you to feel bad or guilty? Have you ever done or said something mean that slights another person? Ever blown up at someone who didn't deserve it? Ever let someone you care about down? If you have done these things and it registered with you as a consequence, then chances are, you were less inclined to repeat them. If you've done these things and still do them, then the consequences you felt were not strong enough to elicit a behavior change.

Triggers are everywhere

In the context of evolution, when we experience a negative emotion such as anger, fear, shame, frustration, or annoyance, we make certain cognitive appraisals, or interpretations, in our heads. When you feel a crap emotion, your brain is telling you that the person or situation that brought it about is a threat.

This made more sense back in caveman days than it does now. If you've ever gotten all gussied up only to have your significant other fail to notice, you may have felt pissed and hurt. He might get the door for you, hold your hand while you're out, smile and be sweet, but you were stuck on the fact that he didn't give you a dang compliment. There was no need for real fear, but your brain didn't seem to know it.

Now, science will tell us that

PART of our IRRATIONAL LUNACY is not entirely our fault.

Let that sink in, people. Part of it is not our fault because "our brains are designed by evolution to focus on and remember the things that are negative, threatening, and blocking us." But the other part is our responsibility to manage.

Hyperfocusing comes naturally

Back in the old school, when peeps experienced the negative feeling of fear, it activated their hyperfocus, which in turn promoted survival. Today the negative feelings that activate our hyperfocusing systems may be, not only fear, but also anger, sadness, jealousy, embarrassment, shame, guilt, anxiety, envy, inferiority, and more.

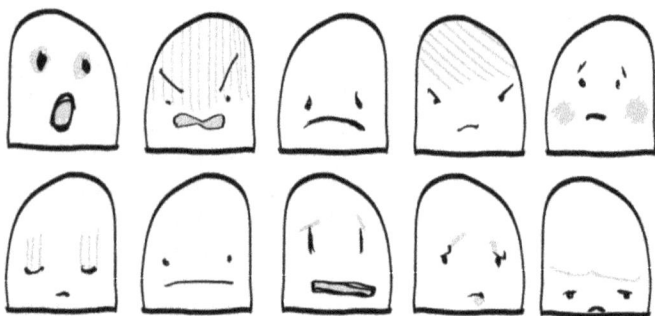

Back in the day, things were less complicated—or to be more accurate, less developed. So just as our civilization has evolved, so too has our psyches, leaving them more vulnerable to erroneous activations. How many cavewomen do you think got bummed out and had their hyperfocusing systems activated because someone stole their parking spot at the market? How many cavemen got pissed because someone at the gym was doing curls in the squat rack?

Chill the heck out

Here are some examples that could cause our modern brain anxiety: the death of a family member, being embarrassed in public, being disliked by a peer. These are "modern" in the sense that they do not physically jeopardize our safety or survival, but are capable of making us feel nervous, bummed, or depressed.

Our modern brain has developed because our survival needs have been met for so long.

*L*EAR*n*i*n*G *to manage* And *R*E*G*u*J*at*e* OUR MODERN BRAIN RES*PONSES* *is where we need the most* HELP

The next chapter will teach you how to manage and regulate these responses so you can learn how to chill the heck out in your own life.

Chapter 5 | How to manage anxiety

Get some perspective

Science tells us that part of our irrational lunacy about fear, anxiety, and hyperfocusing is not our fault. . . but it says the other part is. We are responsible for how we react, and here's a bazillion-dollar lesson: The way to stop hyperfocusing on negative events is to accept that your feelings—even if they are unpleasant—are *valid* and are *communicating something valuable* to you.[1]

The way to accept your unpleasant feelings and move from a feeling state to a thinking state, even when you're revved all the way up, is to broaden your perspective. Remember that just as our bodies evolved from our ancestors, so too did our emotions. If we allow ourselves to get stuck in an anxiety or fear response, we are letting actual nonthreatening events threaten us, and this kind of deforms our natural alarm systems.

Figure out what makes you anxious

Ask yourself what makes you most anxious, then bring that into your awareness. Is it the idea of getting embarrassed in front of others? Of getting fired? Of ending up alone? Of dying? What elicits anxiety in each of us depends upon a number of factors, including the things we were exposed to growing up, our current environment, our temperament and personality, our social development, and our feelings about ourselves. But no matter where your anxiety comes from, if you're ever going to successfully manage it, you need to be able to get some perspective.

When you can't do this and are unable to wrangle up your thoughts, they create future-based anxiety and you waste time living in a worry-laden state. Life passes you by and you throw away precious moments that could be spent experiencing happiness.

Take Kat, who was so anxious and self-conscious that it took her three+ hours to get ready for an evening out with friends, not to mention the time she spent during the week just thinking about it. She worried about being judged by others, about saying something stupid, about falling, about being unhip.

To deal with her anxiety, Kat first had to accept that she was anxious for a good reason. She wanted people to like her (which is natural and normal)—but what she couldn't see was that they already did. We want to feel connected to others because relatedness is a desire we all share. After Kat understood that a big part of her anxiety was related to her desire to be liked and her fear of being disliked, she could begin to accept its presence. Once she nailed the acceptance part, she could start counterbalancing.

Kat had to refute her negative thinking and defeat it, or at least equalize it, so it didn't control her. Gradually she learned how to do this.

First, she had to learn to be mindful of her feelings, then how to relax in their presence. She practiced paying attention to the signs her body gave off when she was becoming anxious. Once she noticed the physical feeling of anxiety and became mindful of it, she implemented breathing exercises. She decided on a 4:6 inhale:exhale ratio (inhale for the count of 4, exhale for the count of 6—we're going to talk more about this later). This was soothing. It lowered her heart rate and enabled her to think in a more rational manner as it moved her out of a feeling state and into a thinking state.

Once Kat had trained herself to pay attention to her anxiety and notice when she was feeling it, she could be more rational. She started reminding herself that she was a nice person. That she was funny, smart, gentle, and sincere. That her group of friends were accepting and that the reality is, you can't please everyone.

Then Kat realized a biggie—the SO WHAT biggie that we can all apply to our lives. *So what* if you say something stupid? *So what* if you lose your balance, trip and fall? *So what* if someone doesn't like your outfit? So. Fucking. What. Seriously? Will the world end? Will you become so devastated that you can't recover from a blow made to your ego by some judgmental asswad? No way. You will recover, and shit happens. We all mess up sometimes. Everyone has different tastes and styles and who cares if some shitbird doesn't think you're cool.

Additionally, if your friends are going to judge you harshly for any of those things, then they're dweebs and jabronis and don't deserve your friendship to begin with.

The big-picture realization that Kat had was that her life wasn't going to stop if some random person didn't like her or think she was cool. When it comes down to it, we all want to be liked by the people we care about, and she already had that—a best friend she's had for 13 years, parents who were super supportive, and siblings who loved her. Once she shifted her frame of mind to be more accepting of the anxiety in order to understand it, she was able to remind herself of these positive aspects and take back some of the power she'd forfeited to other people without her knowledge. This helped to reduce her anxiety even more.

Another thing Kat did was to create reassuring statements she could use when she began to feel anxious. Some noteworthy examples follow.

- "I deserve to be happy."
- "No one is perfect, including me, and that's okay."
- "Thank you, anxiety, for trying to protect me, but you can peace out now."
- "Breathe, baby, breathe, you totally got this."
- "This anxiety is a temporary feeling that will pass."
- "People already do like me, and those who judge me can go suck an egg."
- "Shitbirds and jabronis don't deserve my attention."

These are tricks of the trade, people, and they work. Try them out for yourself and see what happens. Chances are, some good will come out of it.

Accept your emotions for what they are

The awesome power of acceptance does not just apply to anxiety. Its benefits transcend the realm of emotion. So for everyone who is sensitive, or has ever felt down and out, or has ever had their feelings hurt, you must learn to accept that your anger, frustration, irritation, sadness, and distress are normal, and you have a right to feel the way you do.

You must also wrangle up your feelings so they don't go all buck wild on you, and remind yourself that just because you feel upset, it doesn't mean the person you believe triggered your emotion is an evil butthead from Planet Sucko. It just means that maybe someone did or said something that upset you, and that's okay. I mean, yes, maybe they are a dirtbag and you want them out of your life, but if they forgot to ask how your day was, it doesn't mean they're a selfish weenie.

If you feel down and out due to a myriad of reasons not attributed to one person, and as if the situation you're in is hopeless, the same type of logic applies. The way to fight back against all those cruddy feelings and shit thoughts is to (1) *ACCEPT* them and (2) *ACKNOWLEDGE* the big picture. The big picture, meaning you remind yourself that things will not always be this bad, that you do in fact have the power to get out of this funky rut and change your thoughts, and believe it or not, that someone somewhere else has it much worse than you.

Openness shall set you free

If you're going to get rad and stay rad, one hella important part of the process is getting out of denial and staying open to your emotions. I'll turn it over to some very smart guys who did a ton of leg work and found that "... what differentiates psychological health from disordered suffering is not the absence of trauma, pain, and negative private events. The difference is whether people are willing to experience the totality of their psychological and emotional world and still do what matters most to them."[2]

So this means that what separates people with good emotional health from emotionally fucked ones is not the absence of distress, it's the absence of denial. If you can learn and are willing to embrace the whole shebang of your emotions—the good, the bad, and the ugly—then you will be much better off. More mindful, more accepting, and more capable of tolerating your own emotions.

You may be thinking, "Okay, smart guy, my friend, my GF or BF, husband, wife, mom, dad, sister, bruh, etc., has a problem with experiencing too much emotion. They go from zero to bananas lightning fast and are way too emotional."

If that's the case, I would argue that just because they're reactive, it doesn't mean they're in touch with—or even tolerating—the totality of their emotions. I think people who go berserk and fly off the handle or have rapid mood swings can *lack* tolerance; they could be responding that way because they are not accepting their emotions. Just because they are expressive doesn't mean they're connected. It could mean their DLS (deep limbic system) is accustomed to going wild, so when they feel the slightest sensation of stress, anger, sadness, or anxiety, they are reactive.

Learn to tolerate all of your feelings

A big part of being open enough to your emotions to manage them requires that you learn how to better *tolerate* them. This includes the anxiety you have, as well as the other stuff you don't like feeling.

Remember how all your feelings are always okay, all of the time? (Unless you "feel" like you want to hurt yourself, someone else or an animal. . .) Well, this is what I am talking about. And this is not just me blowing ideas out of my ass willy-nilly. Experts Georg Eifert and John Forsyth say that "What makes us human is our capacity to experience a wide range of emotional experience, willingly and without defense, and to adapt and behave effectively despite what we may think or feel. Those who do so willingly and without defense, and adapt and behave effectively despite what they may think or feel, are very healthy indeed"[3]

The key word here is *defense*. When you resist a feeling, it gets more intense. Pardon my grossness, but I'm trying to illustrate an important point here: equate not accepting or tolerating your feelings with the pus that builds inside of a huge ruby-red zit on the chin of an acne-prone teen or the noxious fart smell that flies out of your pooper after a late-night Coney Island binge.

All of your

Emotions are Messengers

and they're not inherently bad. You don't need to be defended against them. They magnify what's going on in your heart and communicate that to your brain, and they can work with you if you lower your guard.

When you feel like running, stay awhile

Here are the biggest ways to increase your emotional tolerance:

1.) Train yourself to be aware of when and how you avoid things.
2.) Tell yourself that if you feel like avoiding something, you probably shouldn't.

I mean this within reason. If you feel like you should avoid petting an alligator that walks into your backyard, it's probable you should. But if you feel like avoiding a conversation with your wife about having kids because the thought of it gives you anxiety, then it's probable you shouldn't.

Psychologists like me help people learn how to pay attention to the times when they feel like running away from an issue or feeling. We support them as they learn how to do the opposite, which is to handle and get the hell through it.

Mindfulness

Mindfulness is the experience of gently noticing[4] how our attention gets hauled off in different directions, and gently guiding it back to the present moment. So for the guy avoiding his wife, mindfulness may translate to the following thought exchange inside his head:

"My wife brought up the topic of kids and there's that sensation of pain in my stomach again. My instinct is to avoid this topic. My instinct is okay. The reason I want to avoid it is because I feel anxiety when I think about having kids. There is more in life I want to do, including getting to a place where I am more settled in my career, before we have kids. My anxiety is a normal human emotion and I accept this without judging myself. My wife is reasonable and will understand where I'm coming from, and even if she doesn't at first, I have to be open and honest about how I feel. I am confident that I can do this. All my emotions are okay, including anxiety."

Now. . . this internal dialogue is pretty advanced, and if this dude is able to have a process along these lines, he is supremely awesome and on his way to mastering his emotions. If he is able to take the reins from the anxiety that wants to hijack his attention and steer it into other areas (like make him avoid it altogether), then he is a total badass. Let's examine his train of thought:

1.) He acknowledges the physical effect of anxiety on his body.
2.) He acknowledges why he feels this way.
3.) He is accepting of the feeling.

Becoming mindful of his anxiety enables him to acknowledge that his anxiety serves a purpose, and this can help him remember that it is one of many normal human emotions. The more he acknowledges his feelings as they happen, the less he'll avoid them.

Allowing yourself to experience the full range of human emotions—and not just what you feel when you're happy, like when you've finished your work week, or right after you nut—is a big part of emotional health. The other part is learning how to manage those emotions. This is what you need to get to some next-level awesomeness.

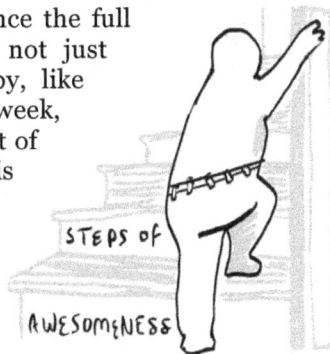

STEPS OF

AWESOMENESS

Avoidance messes up your life (most of the time)

What separates people who are casualties of their past from those who are leaders of their future is the way they handle their emotions.

Based on the way we interpret events, we can either be at the mercy of our emotions or in command of them. Here's a truth bomb that psychologists will drop on you if you come into their office: *Avoidance messes up your life.*

The most difficult thing about avoidance is its insidious nature. It's one enticing minx. All it takes is a single flash of its candy pasties and you're hypnotized (either the food or the booby kind, whichever you prefer). Know why? Because avoidance provides instant gratification, kind of like the short-lived gratification a person would get after eating, say, twelve Oreos in five minutes (not that I've ever done that). The reason avoidance is so dangerous is that **INSTANT GRATIFICATION BRINGS INSTANT REINFORCEMENT**

The Avoidance→ Relief Trap

AVOIDANCE + RELIEF = Reinforcement = ·DEVIL BABY FROM HELL

When you avoid something that feels uncomfortable, you experience relief, and the two form a rapid alliance that brainwashes you into thinking you need them both to feel better. What you need to be mindful of is that the connection comes on strong, like that creepy uncle who hugs you too long while trying to maintain eye contact. When you seek relief through avoidance, you are tricking yourself into feeling good.

Reinforcement is the devil baby born of the unholy union between avoidance and relief.

Consider it your shit prize. It's a prize because you do get actual relief, and it's shit because you don't realize at the time how much damage it can cause in your life. I'm not totally knocking avoidance and relief, because they do serve a purpose, and avoidance is sometimes a healthy thing (which we'll talk about in a bit). But when avoidance does the dirty with relief, the results will drag you way, way, way down.

PRIZE

"Hey, look at that. Just the thought of talking to my boyfriend about how I think he's not living up to his potential made me feel uncomfortable, sooooooo I went shopping instead and bought a bunch of stuff at H&M and Forever 21, and now I feel way better!"

This gal's experience of discomfort led her to avoid an important topic. Instead of sticking with the discomfort and addressing the issue, she avoided it and vested her attention elsewhere by deciding to go buy stuff to gain relief. (Another common avoidance tactic is eating.)

Or how about this scenario:

"Man, I love my girl. She's so cute and nice, but I really wish we had more sex. And kinky sex, too, not just the Blahma Sutra. I don't know what to do because I love her,

but I am not satisfied with our sex life. She's insecure about her body and I don't know what else to do to make her feel more confident. . . I guess I'll just check out other girls, go to titty bars, and masturbate every day to this Jostens class ring catalog."

In this example, this dude's experience of frustration leads him to avoid further discussion of his dissatisfied sex life, and he invests his energy in other outlets because he has a need (a natural and normal need) that he wants to get met one way or other.

The routes these two chose to gain relief are not conducive to healthy coping.

I understand why a person would react this way. I do. I think we're all guilty of falling into this trap and participating in a nasty three-way with unpleasant emotion → avoidance → relief. We often do this unknowingly. I mean, for the girl in the scenario, is it easier to go shopping or to have a conversation with someone she cares about who makes her feel like her stomach is clawing its way up her GI tract 0.00000000001 nanometers at a time? And for the guy, broaching the sexy-time dissatisfaction topic with his girl could get her upset and make her feel even more self-conscious, which in turn makes him feel like garbage water. Talking about this could force him to realize that maybe this issue is a deal-breaker for him, and that he needs to assess whether they can last in the long run. Heavy shit.

I'm not suggesting that you break up with your partner if he or she has an insecurity, but sometimes you may be avoiding a topic because deep down you know what the implications are, and you want to put off dealing with it. Unfortunately, the longer you put it off, the worse it gets.

We often don't even realize avoidance has snuck into our lives because the relief we feel blinds us. And how can we not be blinded? Relief trumps a lot of other emotions. Just think about how good you feel when you find out something that alleviates your concern.

When you find out you didn't leave your credit card at that seedy gas station downtown. When you find out your sister-in-law's cancer is in full remission. When you find out that your husband is not face down, ass up in an alley somewhere on the other side of the world, and the reason he didn't call you when he got to Melbourne was that his phone battery died.

Healthy Avoidance—get back here, relief, I need you!

I know I made it seem like avoidance is what would happen if a tumor and a piece of doo-doo had a baby, BUT avoidance isn't alllll bad. The trouble is that it can be quite hard to determine whether it's healthy or toxic. It can be healthy when you use it to cope with the death of a loved one or the end to a romantic relationship (which is a death of sorts). As you vacillate through the stages of grief (denial, anger, bargaining, depression, and acceptance5), distracting yourself can be a good thing. It helps you take a mental break from the emotional pain as you heal. The issue is still there, but avoiding it by going back to work, talking to your friends again, taking a shower, or watching a movie helps you catch your breath.

The trick is to *MAKE SURE YOU DON'T USE AVOIDANCE to the point that You DROWN OUT oTHER feelings*

Remember, you have to allow yourself to actually feel all your feelings: the good, the bad, and the ugly. That's what healthy is, and that's what will help you cultivate greater emotional well-being. When you allow yourself to feel, you are nourishing your psyche. Every time you let yourself experience the totality of your emotions, think of it as feeding your psyche the fruits and veggies it needs to stay awesome.

for A HEALTHY PSYCHE

Remaining mindful of your feelings and accepting and tolerating them when they pierce your awareness nourishes your mental health and emotional well-being so you can stay healthy.

So for the gal that's bummed because the dude she loves is stuck and not living up to his potential, she needs to let herself acknowledge feeling bummed, and not run away from it. If she is going to have an honest relationship, she will need to address the issue with him (sooner rather than later) , so they can have an open dialogue about it. Same goes for the guy who loves his girl but is not keen on their lack of coitus. He will need to address the issue head on (no pun intended). If he doesn't, he is letting avoidance overpower and drown out his true feelings of frustration, disappointment, and probable anger. These feelings are okay, but they need to be addressed before they morph into a resentment ball or devil baby.

Put your avoidance on a diet

If you have been paying attention, you can see that using avoidance to the point where it chokes out your other feelings is no bueno. You know now that the relief you feel might be a façade, because it gives you the illusion that the issue is dealt with, when in reality, it has grown worse. Excessive use of avoidance robs you of the opportunity to prove to yourself that you can deal with unpleasant feelings and emotions, and it keeps you from developing a tolerance for stuff you need to learn to tolerate.

Cutting down on avoidance means being mindful and noticing when you're using it. It means getting comfortable calling yourself out because you realize that copping to the shitty shit you do is a part of growth. It means acknowledging that not bringing up an important topic with someone you love is a huge disservice to you and your relationship because it creates distance. It means being confident enough to realize that facing an issue you want to avoid can in fact be done, and that doing so will not cause a wormhole in the universe. And it means understanding that if we never fall, we never learn to pick ourselves up.

Ya gotta show yourself some love

Being compassionate toward yourself will help you cope with anxiety and other unpleasant feelings. Here are some tips to help you be kinder to yourself:

1.) Acknowledge that struggling with anxiety causes you distress and keeps you from feeling more calm and content.
2.) Believe that if you come to terms with the feelings you don't like having, your life will be better.
3.) Be open to experiencing sympathy toward yourself as you make attempts to cope with your emotions in healthier ways.

Serve yourself up some compassionate sympathy

When you are in tune with your own emotions of anxiety and discomfort, practicing compassionate sympathy will help you cope and do something positive about it.

Sympathy stands in direct opposition to anger. When we respond to our yucky feelings with sympathy instead of anger or frustration, we protect ourselves from further distress.

Responding with compassion

1.) gives you permission to feel what you feel,
2.) teaches you there are gentler ways of coping with your feelings, and
3.) demonstrates that you don't have to needlessly suffer.

Create positive self-statements

It can be easy to have compassion for others, but we may not grant ourselves the same clemency. Finding positive self-statements or affirmations, which convey that you deserve sympathy, kindness, and compassion and are worthy of happiness, is a good exercise to do. This was part of Kat's strategy at the beginning of the chapter. Recall the "I deserve to be happy," "No one is perfect, including me, and that's okay," and "Breathe, baby, breathe, you totally got this," statements. These affirmations promote compassion and are encouraging.

EXERCISE for ya BRAIN

Think about something that bums you out or makes you feel bad about yourself, then scan that magnificent brain of yours and come up with at least three positive things to say to yourself— things that reflect compassion and are encouraging to you. I bet if I knew you I'd be able to name more than twenty right off the bat, but a lot of times it's like pulling gnarly teeth to do something like this for yourself. However, since you're being given gentle instructions to do so now, please create at least three meaningful statements that help you feel relief, that you can repeat when you feel down or anxious or not good enough.

I'll start it off, and no double-dipping, you can't use mine.

1.) I am just as deserving of love as anyone else on this planet.
2.) The things I struggle with are not abnormal, and everyone struggles sometimes.
3.) I will show myself the kindness I so easily grant to others.

Now your turn.

1 _____

2 _____

3 _____

Conclusion

If the human race can build spaceships, explore planets, find cures for diseases, transplant organs, and create new forms of technology, don't you think you are at least capable of accepting and tolerating your emotions? And don't you think you can learn how to use less avoidance and instead deal with your emotions when you want to tear ass faster than a coked-out cheetah? These, my dear friend, are skills you can no doubt learn. You don't have to understand aerospace engineering, how the internet works, or what the hell nougat is. You just have to work at being more accepting, tolerant, and mindful of your feelings and emotions—and call yourself out so you put the kibosh on avoidance tactics, and see through the false relief it tricks you into feeling. You can learn to master your emotions if you are receptive to them and are mindful, accepting, and tolerant of their existence. Believe in yourself, take responsibility, and make a positive change. Because you can.

Part II: AWESOMENESS

Chapter 6 | Get Rad

In the first half of this book, BEING, I spent time telling you why attachment is important and what you need to do to get rid of the bunk thoughts that keep you down. I talked about depression and explained what it is and how you can stop it. And I showed you that anxiety is normal and established that it is possible to make peace with it. In the last half, AWESOMENESS, we're going to talk about self-awareness, self-management, and how people change. These concepts and ideas are so ballz-out amazing, they warrant their own section. Round two, here we go.

Self-awareness

What exactly is self-awareness, and why is it so rad?

Basically, being self-aware comes from looking inwards at yourself. It's taking a magnifying glass to your behavior, habits, and tendencies, and identifying to what your thoughts and emotions are connected to. People who are self-aware recognize that they are individuals with autonomy who are separate from others, and they accept responsibility for their actions.

When you are self-aware, you are conscious of several things:

1.) your emotions, your drives, your desires, and your motives,
2.) the thoughts you have when you experience #1, and
3.) the behaviors that accompany #1 & #2.

A brilliant thing about self-awareness is that just by thinking about it, you become self-aware.

MAJOR POINTIOLA:

Self-awareness Enables you To ACTUALLY Control Your CONSCIOUSNESS,

How to become self-aware

All people are unique, different, and peculiar in their own way, but at the same time, we are the same. Our experiences do not deviate too far from each other's, so the process of self-discovery is similar in all of us. Whether you're the Queen of Naboo, super-sexy Christian Bale, Marshall Mathers, or a nine-to-fiver busting your butt five days a week to make ends meet, if you are going to gain self-awareness, your process and everyone else's follow similar trajectories.

The good news for you ladies and gents is that gaining self-awareness ain't that hard. If you can walk and talk, if you can poop and pee, if you can bump and grind, then you can learn to be self-aware. Here's how:

1.) Learn how to perceive your emotions as they occur.
2.) Understand your general pattern of behavior and how you tend to react.[1]

Play "How does that make you feel?" with yourself (a nonsexual game)

Remember in elementary school when you had to match a word to a sentence? That's one of the things you're doing when you build self-awareness: trying to link the emotions you are having in a given moment to your thought processes, then later identifying how those thoughts and emotions influenced your behavior.

In the examples below, I'll ask you to link the thought process or event to the emotion you think it generates.

Dani didn't call me today and I really wanted her to.	Happy
I overate so I feel like shit.	Afraid
My mom and I spent the day together and we had fun.	Sad
Doctors found an abnormal growth on my grandpa's lung and it might be cancer.	Ashamed

The only way to become more familiar with the internal workings of that beautiful mind of yours is to spend time thinking about your emotions, and identifying the thoughts and behaviors that accompany them. Since our brains work by bringing an emotion into our awareness before our rational thought enters the scene (recall the 101 biology from Chapter 2), it is important to learn about your emotions so they don't end up taking you hostage.

I know this sounds campy and all psychology-schmychology of me, but seriously, the ol "How does that make you feel?" line clinicians like me use, is a total keeper. You need to start asking yourself that question multiple times a day if you want to gain self-awareness.

Emotions are super!

Our emotions are super fantastical because they are both messengers and teachers. They're messengers in the sense that they communicate something to us about our experiences. Don't forget that *emotions always come from somewhere.* Even if you feel like one just popped out of thin air, it didn't, and if you think long enough, it's probable you can figure out what triggered it.

Our emotions are also teachers in the sense that they educate us on, well, just that... us. They enable us to gain personal insight. If you can learn to pay attention to what they're trying to tell you, you're well on your way to being a self-aware, self-informed, self-enlightened badass. Self-awareness teaches you how to listen to what those sweet emooooootions (à la Steven Tyler) are communicating.

How to get rad once and for all

Now that you understand what self-awareness is, I'll serve you up some tangible ways to increase it. Two super smart fellas, Travis Bradberry and Jean Greaves, outlined specific ways to help people increase their self-awareness in their book *Emotional Intelligence.* Following these eight solutions is a foolproof way to help you get rad. If you want to stay rad, you have to practice them on the reg.

GET RAD PRINCIPLE 1—
STOP TREATING YOUR EMOTIONS AS ONLY GOOD OR BAD.

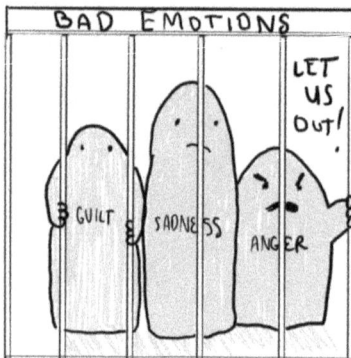

These are boring, linear, binary groups. If you only see your emotions in black and white, you may avoid feeling anger, guilt, and sadness, and solely seek joy and excitement. The former emotions may make you feel bad to a certain extent, but if you deny them or try to avoid feeling them, they become more powerful.

Those negative emotions are there to communicate something meaningful to you. Listen to what they're trying to say.

All your emotions are always okay all of the time

I know using the words "always" and "never" should be done with extreme caution. And I know that feeling and acting on our emotions are two separate phenomena.

All your emotions are always okay all of the time, means that you allow yourself to feel whatever it is you actually feel, and don't try to deny it. Folks often have the hardest time feeling their feelings when it comes to experiencing a hurtful or "negative" emotion toward someone they love—annoyance toward a child, anger toward a best friend, disappointment toward a spouse. If you've ever said to yourself, "God, I love her so much and I would punch out anyone that ever hurt her, but sometimes that woman can drive me batshit crazy," then you know what I mean.

Although simultaneously having positive and negative feelings about the same person is normal, it can make you uneasy. I suggest you try not to deny it. Instead simply listen to it, explore it within yourself, investigate what it means, and learn effective management of the negative feelings when they come around. The truth is, if you've never felt annoyed or angry at someone you love, how deep can the relationship really be? But if those negative feelings dominate the relationship... that's a different story.

GET RAD PRINCIPLE 2—OBSERVE THE WAY YOU ACT OUT YOUR EMOTIONS AND THE RIPPLE EFFECT THAT HAS ON OTHERS.

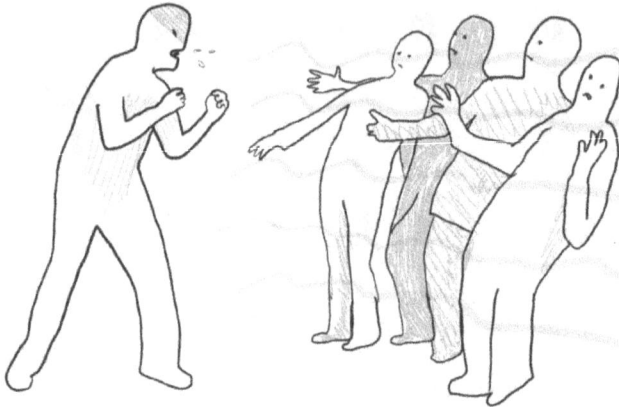

Since emotions influence and drive our behavior, it is worth examining the effects yours have on others. This comes in handy in relationships because it helps you build your empathy skills and perspective-taking abilities.

A big chunk of my job is helping people see the impact their emotions have on their own lives. Getting in touch with the emotional side of you takes practice. It's a process that can be hella easy, though, because

ALL YOU HAVE TO DO IS NOTICE

Notice how you show certain emotions to certain others. **Notice** how your friend or partner or parent or coworker responds to you when you are in a certain mood. **Notice** their body language when you're pissed, sad, or angry. **Notice** how you respond to that. **Notice** your tone and how it impacts the dynamic. **Notice** what they do in response to the way you exhibit your emotion.

Do they try to understand when you express yourself? Do they back off or get angry? What do they do in response to you? These are important questions to ask because they help you cultivate a deepened understanding of the effects your emotions have. Asking yourself these questions increases your self-awareness.

Think of the last time you interacted with someone when you felt angry. What did your anger look like? How did you express it? Were you verbal? If so, what did you say? How did the other party react to you? What do you think was going on in their mind? What would have been going on in your mind if you saw someone react the way you did?

Maybe you expressed your anger in a nonverbal way. If so, how did you act? What did you do? What message did you give off? What do you think the other party gathered from your demeanor? What do you think their impression was of you? What would have been your impression of someone who reacted the way you did to feeling angry?

Looking outside of yourself to identify the effects you have on others gives you a more comprehensive understanding of your emotional states. It adds a new dimension to your experience and takes you to the next level of awesomeness. This is because integrating other people's reactions to us takes advanced-level processing. It requires us to be honest and lower our defenses, so we can allow ourselves to understand another person's perspective. It may be tricky at first, because we all have defenses, but if you're going to grow and increase self-awareness, it's gotta be done.

Because if a girl like me, who once searched her car for her missing cell phone *whilst* she was talking on it, can become self-aware, there is no doubt in my mind that you can, too.

GET RAD PRINCIPLE 3—LEAN INTO DISCOMFORT TO INCREASE SELF-AWARENESS.

It's normal for us to avoid things we don't like, but you need to turn toward the discomfort you feel if you want to gain self-awareness and achieve personal growth. When you get that icky feeling in the pit of your stomach, you need to stay right there and try to understand what's going on. Doing this is coping—the opposite of avoiding.

Repetition raises your tolerance for distress, which means you're becoming more capable of enduring painful and upsetting life events, which in the long run will serve you very, very well.

When we feel discomfort, many of us want to blast that fucker in the face and eliminate it at once, but doing so will just make things worse. You also can't ignore it, because if you do, it gets stronger and you get weaker. So if you're not supposed to nix it right away or avoid it, then what the heck do you do?

Answer: You let the discomfort be and learn how to coexist with it.

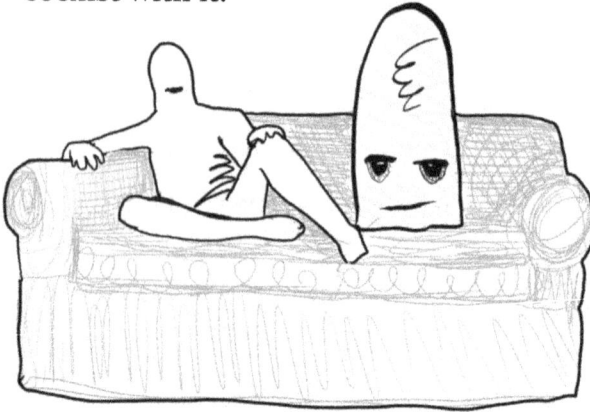

You can practice by thinking of something that makes you feel uncomfortable, then allowing yourself to experience being uncomfortable . Whether it's a conversation you need to have with your mate, feelings of impending doom because of a big project coming due, or feelings of anxiety about death, just let yourself sit with it.

I'm not saying you should succumb to it. What I'm saying is that when you bring the unpleasant issue into that beautiful consciousness of yours, let it stick around so it becomes less scary and more tolerable. Even if you have to set a timer and stop at thirty seconds, see how much of a particular discomforting thought you can tolerate, and allow yourself a gradual experience of the emotions that follow. Easing your way into these feelings will hopefully prove to you that you can in fact tolerate them, and will confirm that you do experience relief after you lean into the discomfort instead of avoiding it.

Avoidance gives a mere illusion of relief. You can use all sorts of maladaptive avoidance strategies with that mind of yours, but they will come back to bite you hard in the ass. And

I'm talking about a really huge, hard, mastodon-sized bite.

The trick here is to

JUST SIT
with the
DISCOMFORT

until you're okay with it. You'll find that the world doesn't end, you'll survive, and it's tolerable.

GET RAD PRINCIPLE 4—LEARN TO FEEL YOUR EMOTIONS PHYSICALLY.

The mind-body connection is no joke, people. When you experience an emotion, electrical signals are launched through your brain, which then trigger physical sensations in your body.

In order to familiarize yourself with the physical effects your emotions have on you, try this exercise: Clear your head and focus on your breathing. Feel your heartbeat and notice the pace at which it beats. Notice your breathing patterns and how tense or relaxed are the muscles in your face. How tense or relaxed are the muscles in your stomach? In your arms? In your legs?

Now, I'll ask you to think of two events in your life. The first is one that evokes strong feelings of happiness, something so positive that it fills your heart with love and joy when you think of it. Let that memory wash over you and sit with it. How does your body feel when you remember this?

Pause.

Pause.

Pause.

Experience it. Feel your body's physical sensations when this memory comes to life in your awareness.

Now let's do the opposite. Think of an event that evokes sadness or pain. Be with that memory.

Pause.

Pause.

Pause.

Experience it. What do you feel now? Notice the physical changes to your body. Did your heart rate change or stay the same? How about your breathing—what happened to it? What about your muscles; did you encounter more tension in certain areas? How do your stomach and chest feel?

Envisioning these events and recognizing the different physical effects they have on you will help you tune in to the merging of body and mind that goes on when we experience strong emotional reactions.

GET RAD PRINCIPLE 5—KNOW WHAT PUSHES YOUR BUTTONS.

Understanding this principle requires you to spend time bringing the situations, people, and topics that elicit strong emotions into your awareness. To be aware of the things that make you go hmmmm and the things that make you want to scream, cringe, and projectile vomit everywhere.

Notice what happens when you bring a person or situation that makes you recoil in disgust into your awareness. What do you feel? What happens to your insides when you think of something that's kind of a shitstain on life?

Thinking about this stuff is not a punishment, but an investment in your sanity. You have to figure out what this reaction is all about. Are you threatened? Did someone make you feel inferior? Are you perturbed by their arrogance? Enraged by their ignorance?

Asking yourself these questions and figuring out the answers is one of the first steps toward enhancing your coping skills. It raises your awareness, which will help you understand how to manage the muck feelings in a successful way.

After you explore your hot buttons and the people or circumstances pushing them, the goal is to find a connection. For example, you may realize that the annoying guy at work (who's not really annoying) reminds you of your bozo ex, who carried himself in a similar way, and that's why he bugs you. Being around this coworker who had nothing to do with your breakup may still trigger you to feel angry or defensive.

Another example would be coming to understand that when you perceive someone acting passive-aggressively, it sets you off faster than a bottle rocket laced with dynamite because your mom used dysfunctional communication like this when you were growing up.

Anytime something has the power to set you off, it'll behoove you to

stop, collaborate
(with your emotions and thoughts)

and listen
(to what they are telling you). You are having a big reaction for a good reason. These emotional antecedents didn't come from hell, they were born out of the depths of your past. Finding the connection between your current hot-button issue and its original source will make it easier for you to manage your emotion, let go of unhealthy responses, and be less reactive.

Sometimes it takes an ocean not to break

Thinking about the things and people that piss you off and trigger hostile emotions can be an empowering experience, because it enables something magnificent to occur—it lets you understand yourself better. Understanding yourself better gives you more control in your life and keeps you from being a helpless victim of your circumstance. **If you are aware of who pushes your buttons and why they have this effect on you,** you can take steps to prepare yourself for the reaction you may have.

For example, a young woman I know had a real problem with girls who flirted with men who were already in relationships. Even though she felt secure with her partner of two years, she came to realize that these women held some serious influence over her. They held the power* to make her feel threatened and inferior, and she became defensive and angry at the thought of someone flirting with her boyfriend. When she explored this, she hit upon some valid insecurities and fears.

In time she came to realize that these women triggered doubts she had about herself, which made her feel vulnerable and made her think about trust issues in her relationship. Once she had a better understanding of her hot-button issue, these women were less threatening.

*The devil made me do it

Be careful with the inclination to use the word "make" in the example above: ". . . they held the power to make her feel threatened and inferior." Saying someone "makes" you feel a certain way can be dangerous if you have not gained a true understanding of your emotions. You could see the word "make" and think it implies force, which is not the case at all. No one forces you to feel a certain way. The better understanding is that

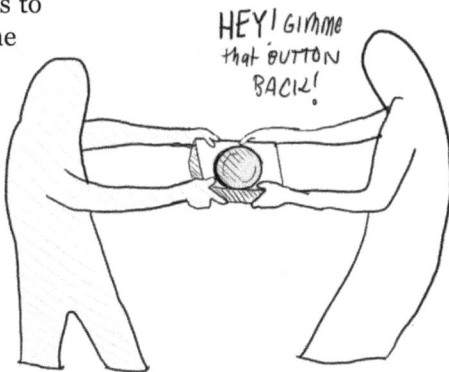

you are allowing yourself to be influenced by this person's behavior in such a way that it activates certain emotions within you.

WE ARE RESPONSIBLE for the way we allow others to Affect US

The young woman who gets upset just thinking about a hypothetical girl flirting with her partner is allowing the other person to influence her. Vulnerability is a scary thing and it takes time to understand how to cope with it when it's triggered. Realizing how other people have the power to affect you—and that you are ultimately in charge of that influence—is a great place to start.

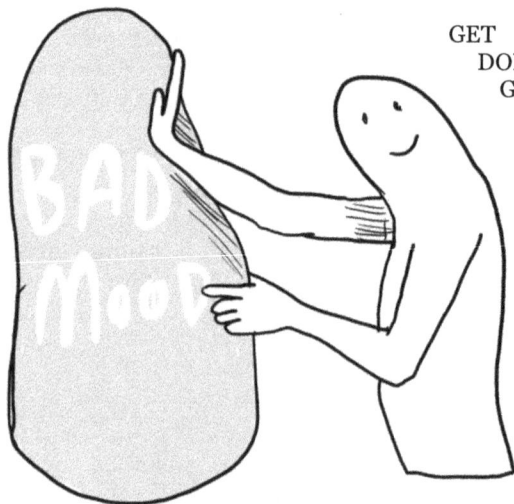

GET RAD PRINCIPLE 6— DON'T LET A BAD MOOD GET THE BEST OF YOU.

Getting stung by a bad mood happens to all of us some time or other, and when it does, try reminding yourself that (1) everything will not always be this bad, and that (2) you still have a lot of things in your life to feel happy about.

I know this is hard to do when you are stuck in the gutter and feeling super down. But at some point, if you're ever going to ditch the shit feelings for better ones, you have to try to remind yourself that numbers 1 and 2 above are a reality.

An important part of self-awareness is being able to identify your emotions and knowing what you're going through, even if you can't change it at the time. Not letting a bad mood spread through your emotional state like wildfire, ties into combating the eleven dysfunctional thoughts we outlined in Chapter 3. There are elements of all-or-nothing thinking, overgeneralizing, mental filters, disqualifying the positive, and magnification going on when we let a bad mood get the best of us, and they keep us from seeing the big picture.

So when you notice yourself feeling bad, identify the feeling for what it is—an emotion that is coming from somewhere and has a reason for being there—then tell yourself that

even though this is how you feel right now, It will not always be this way.

Remind yourself that your dumpy feelings are not permanent, and that you are taking steps to change your situation. (If you're not taking steps to change it, then start taking those steps. I'll show you how in the last chapter.)

Remember that all your feelings are okay, and all you can do is cope with them as well as possible. Also remember that your brain has the awesome power to control your consciousness, and all it takes is self-awareness.

Regardless of where you are on the "taking action to change your life" continuum, repeat this to yourself when you feel down and you need motivation: *My emotions change all the time, and this bad mood will pass if I let it.*

This is the truth, so let it sink in. If this kind of statement sounds like dog shit to you as you read it, then you may be more depressed (or angry, or distraught) than you realize.

Digging out of that funky rut when you feel like a steaming pile of hot garbage means the next time you feel crappy, sad, down, melancholy, rejected,

lonely, glum, gloomy, miserable, forlorn, somber, desolate, troubled, morose, depressed, or sepulchral, try balancing out your thoughts by reminding yourself of all the successes, accomplishments, loving relationships, and positive things in your life. And by reminding yourself that your shit feelings do not have to be permanent. And that you have the power to change your thinking and your mood.

Take some time here and think about the things in your life you have to be grateful for. Identify at least five things. If you're unable to identify any positive aspects of your life at all, then you may need to talk to a licensed clinician.

Only the lonely

A common bad-mood inducer I hear in my office is from people out there who are lonely and sad because they don't have someone special to share their life with. If you fall into this category, my advice is to remind yourself of the positive things you are doing to change your situation. If meeting someone is an objective of yours, hopes are you're active in taking steps to find him or her. If you are putting yourself out there by going to your friends' parties, creating an online dating profile, or by being ultra gutsy and giving your phone number to someone you are attracted to, then you get an A+. If you're not taking action, then you're really not going to change your situation, are ya?

Taking action is possible when we start to let some of our rational thoughts in, such as, "I'm self-conscious and have never given a guy my number, but. . . WTF, I've got nothing to lose, and if he doesn't call me, it's not the end of the world! I'm brave for giving it a shot, and that makes me a badass."

Additionally, if you are lonesome, I encourage you to develop your very own special hobbies and interests. Fall in love with yourself. Not in a narcissistic sort of way, but in a healthy, I'm-pretty-fucking-spectacular sort of way. Spend time thinking about what you love to do. What are you interested in? What do you want to learn more about? What brings you joy? Try taking a class, reading a book, going to a movie or on a trip by yourself. By spending your time in constructive pursuits and focusing on yourself, you're more equipped to ward off bad moods. Yes, loneliness is a normal feeling to have sometimes, and being alone all the time blows, but doing stuff you enjoy is a remedy that can teach or remind you that you're solid gold as is.

If you're sitting at home in your sweatpants every weekend and turning down invitations from your friends so you can pig out on Spam and cheese sandwiches and watch *Encino Man* for the umpteenth time, then you're not taking steps to change a circumstance you're not supposed to like. I know bad moods can be immobilizing, so I promise I'm not making fun of you. I love hanging in my sweaties, too. I'm just saying that you have to act if you want to see a change.

GET RAD PRINCIPLE 7—ASK YOURSELF WHAT COMPELS YOU TO DO THE THINGS YOU DO.

There is so much to be gained by discovering why you do the things you do. Asking yourself what motivates you to behave, think, and say the things you do will help you increase your self-awareness. What are you hoping to get by acting, thinking, talking, and even dressing the way you do? Is it respect? Friendship? A laugh? Validation? The answers to these questions exemplify why I love people so much. We are all so different, yet at the exact same time, quite identical.

Research shows that aspiration directs motivation. Our desire to effect positive change in our lives is what compels us humanoids to act.[2] Two lovely gents by the names of Richard Ryan and Edward Deci spent time researching a thing

called self-determination theory and discovered that there are three innate universal needs found in humans.[3] Please bear with my scientifickiness, because this is important.

These dudes found that the desire for **autonomy** (independence and freedom), **relatedness** (being connected to others) and **competency** (being good at something)—or ARC, as they called it—are pretty much what guide our behavior. I want to spend a little more time here because it's important to understand that everyone, including movie stars, rock stars, sport stars, people who study stars in the sky, teachers, doctors, lawyers, social workers, factory employees, bank tellers, graphic designers, editors, producers, anchormen (and women), parks and rec staff, GE executives, and other workaholics all have this in common.

This is super important to discuss because shitty problems develop out of an individual's lack of any or all of ARC. Kids who are smothered by overindulgent parents, like the ones who buy their eight-year-olds iPhones, may be at a disadvantage when it comes to experiencing **autonomy** because they get things handed to them. People who are bullied may not succeed in fulfilling their need for **relatedness** because they are ostracized. And **competency** may not be reached if someone does not develop the belief that they are capable of accomplishing the goals they set.

Autonomy

The common desire for autonomy in affect means that

> AS GROWN-ASS HUMAN BEINGS, we
> All WANT TO FEEL LIKE WE ARE IN CHARGE
> of MAKING the DECISIONS THAT GUIDE OUR LIVES

Think of the biggies: picking your partner, choosing a career and a place to live, deciding whether or not to have children. We all want to feel like we have a say in the most significant aspects of our lives.

So if you feel like you have made a major life decision based on appeasing someone else, I encourage you to reevaluate that choice. Pause for a moment and ask yourself if anything comes to mind that may fit this bill. Why did you pick the career you have? Or the partner you have? Did you select them under pressure to please someone else? "Someone" could be as specific as your mom or dad, or as elusive as society, maybe because you hit a certain age and thought you needed to be married.

To clarify, it is okay to put the needs of others before yours sometimes; that means you're not self-centered. Going to see a band you don't appreciate but your girlfriend loves, working some overtime to help your stepdaughter pay for college classes. . . these are sacrifices you make to please the people you love. But if you make constant sacrifices for others without getting something back—like recognition, validation, or acts of kindness returned—then you might end up feeling taken for granted and used. Make sure you're getting some niceness back.

The whammies that hold a lot of weight, like relationships, career choice, and whether or not to have children are decisions that should come straight from within you. If they don't, you'll set yourself up for disappointment, regret, and heartache in the long run.

Knowing why you are making a decision takes practice and requires you to be aware of your feelings and in tune with your wants and needs. It's a know-thyself-and-to-thine-own-self-be-true kinda thing.

Relatedness

The need for relatedness refers to our connections with the people in our lives. Our parents, siblings, grandparents, partners, and friends are often the people we value most and the ones with which we feel the need to have an authentic bond. Some folks have strong affinities for famous people, but that's not what I'm talking about here. I'm talking about the real people in your real life. These are the ones to cultivate meaningful relationships with, because they're the ones you can experience life with.

Spend time with the people you care about most and the people who care about you. Go ask somebody for a damn hug and let that goodness wash over you like the warm, healing cleanse that it can be. If you're not in touch with your family so much, get at your BFFs for a hug, because they are family and the bonds you share with them may even be thicker than blood.

If you don't yet have this kind of relationship with family or friends, you can create a meaningful bond with a person in need. I volunteer with an amazing organization that serves developmentally disabled adults in my community, and I know there are many local organizations that could use your help. If you're looking to feel an added sense of relatedness, just do a little research and get connected to the right group for you. Create opportunities for yourself to feel connected. They are out there and it can really do ya some good.

If you have already developed an authentic bond with someone, the meaning and fulfillment are ripe for the picking.

All you have to do IS ALLOW YOURSELF to FEEL connected.

Enjoy the company of the people you love when you're with them and allow yourself to experience a sense of relatedness. Pause and take in some of the goodness that is around you, some of the love that people are showing, and some of their kindness. Life ain't so bad. We're all blood and guts on the inside, and we all have a need to connect.

Competence

Last is your need for competence.

WE ALL WANT TO FEEL like we are CAPABLE of MAKING GOOD CHOICES

We want to feel a sense of mastery and to accomplish something meaningful. You can find this in your romantic, familial, or platonic relationships, in your work or your hobbies. Maybe you work as a store manager, but your true passion is playing music or designing clothes or cooking; if you spend time practicing what you love and become competent at it, you'll encourage your sense of self-worth and self-confidence. You can become a competent friend or partner by being a good listener, being supportive, and being available when someone you care about is in need. It's win-win. Gaining experience with the things that add meaning to your life is a surefire way to fulfill your need for competence.

Finding meaning in your life is a personal experience, and what's meaningful for me is not necessarily meaningful for you. If you're going to change for the better and be the most awesomest version of yourself possible, then you have to find some healthy ways to do it. If you want to spend time shopping, it's easy to be competent at that: Spend money + make a purchase = experience success. I'm encouraging you to do something a bit more significant: help a neighbor, take a class, start a hobby, volunteer with an animal shelter or nonprofit.

Although we represent magnificent diversity, we all want to feel autonomous, related, and competent. Now that you know what motivates you on a fundamental level, the simple act of asking yourself "Why do I do the things I do?" will increase your self-awareness. Keep asking yourself questions like this, and you'll better understand how to meet your needs and attain awesomeness.

But be smart about it, okay? Don't drink a 40-oz. before work because you "want to," to achieve autonomy. Don't hook up with a turdbucket ex to achieve relatedness. And don't master ignorance by being a competent douchebag. If you can make good choices about this, you'll be well on your way to getting rad and staying rad.

GET RAD PRINCIPLE 8—
SEEK FEEDBACK.

There is a difference between the way we see ourselves and the way others perceive us at times.   Hopefully there is not too much of a discrepancy, and that the people who know you best have some unanimity of opinion when it comes to the kind of person you are. The reality is that other people see things in us we can't, because of the filters we have in place.

Asking for feedback from individuals we trust and value— and who know us well—is a powerful thing. Being able to receive that feedback is even more powerful because it signifies strength and maturity. I know this because in my past I wasn't stoked on asking for feedback on my personal life, especially when I knew I wasn't going to get the response I wanted. Academically, I was the opposite. I always wanted feedback so I could know how to improve, be a better student and clinician, but feedback of a personal nature? Nuh uh. Keep it to yourself, dude, unless of course you don't plan on questioning my behavior.

A man I once worked with was so worried about my feedback that it took him three months to tell me he quit his job. A good rule of thumb is that if you are guarded against receiving feedback from someone you respect, it could be because you're conflicted and unsettled about it, which is all the more reason to get it out of your system and discuss it. Our defenses can reveal a lot to us, and if you can lower them just enough to accept someone else's point of view (without losing your marbles), it is a sign of fortitude.

That's not to say that the other person's feedback exemplifies implicit correctness, or that you have to apply it to your life. Not at all. What I'm saying is that if you can tolerate hearing comments and observations on your behavior, it's proof that you are becoming more emotionally adept and self-aware.

So if you find that you are the way I used to be, search inside and gather up the courage you need to be brave, then (clench your sphincter and...) brace for that feedback. If you frame asking for input from others in a positive way, a way that communicates to you, "If I do ask for feedback, I will gain self-awareness," then you will see that it's an actual valuable opportunity for you to gain something meaningful. Being able to integrate other people's perspectives into your own enables you to see a more accurate and complete picture, instead of just the world through your lenses.

Think of how someone you know and love would respond if you asked them this question: "When I get stressed out, what is your experience of me?"

Accepting the answer means you're ready to manage your emotional responses and are prepared to debunk the stinkin thinkin or irrational views that might take place after you hear a reply like, "Well, you kind of turn into a spazzy jerk."

If you are self-aware, you won't plunge into a shame spiral or aggro ball. You may feel an ouch to your ego, but with your increased self-awareness, you will be able to remind yourself that "Hey, nobody is perfect, and I can kind of be a spazzy jerk sometimes. I can use this to learn about myself and I will not slip into a downward spiral. Person X was just being honest, and I know they love me."

Asking for feedback enables you to see the way the world experiences you, so go out and get dat feedback, mang. The truth is, you have nothing to be afraid of. You are not perfect, but you are a badass.

Chapter 7 | Stay Rad

Although increasing your level of self-awareness is super duper mega important, you're going to need a little more umph than the previous chapters have let on. We'll talk next about some practical tools that make it easier to manage the newfound glory and wisdom that accompanies increased self-awareness, which—if you're practicing the eight GET RAD principles from the last chapter—you'll soon be poised to seize. To ensure you know how to do this, I'm going to give you the specific tools you need to STAY RAD.

Self-management

Self-management is a subsidiary of self-awareness, kind of like the VP or assistant director. It refers to your ability to tune in to your emotions so you can make active choices about what you say and do. When you stay emotionally aware and flexible in the circumstances you experience, you are self-managing.[1]

You are self-managing when you use an awareness of your emotions in real time to decide how to behave, what to say, and how to react. Sounds pretty rad, right?!

DID YOU KNOW
that as an adult you have
CONTROL AND POWER OVER
YOURSELF?

Over the way you think, behave, react, and respond to people, situations, and circumstances?

This is something I strive to convey to the folks I work with, and I need you to wrap your sexy brain around it, too: *While we cannot always control what happens to us in life, we can control the way we allow ourselves to react to it.* The key to this control is self-management, and the key to self-management is self-awareness (at which you're already a mini pro because of what you learned in the previous chapter). The harsh reality here is that if you don't put the effort into excavating the self-awareness you need to manage your emotional states, then you are in essence handing over your self-control and becoming a victim of emotional hijacking.

I use the word "control" when referring to lassoing up your emotions, but I don't want you to think it implies any type of negative force, since not all force is negative. Think of parents using control to help their children. Sometimes our emotions want what they want and don't respond to reason right away, but that doesn't mean they should get away with it. So, just like you wouldn't let your kid eat ice cream for dinner every night, it's hoped you wouldn't let your emotions start punching matches every time you get pissed. Improving your self-control is a process where you teach your feelings, thoughts, behaviors, and reactions to stop fighting with each other and start cooperating. I want your process to be a gentle and compassionate one. If you're not there yet, you might need a little emergency self-management from time to time.

Emergency self-management—for use in extreme conditions

Say, for instance, you see a girl who is younger and thinner than you—or if you're a guy, a dude who's more muscley and drives a better car (pardon the blazing stereotypes). If you do not spiral down a path of personal debasement and abhorrence when you see this person, and instead are able to acknowledge your own emotions and any insecurity stirred up, you're on your way to self-management. After you tune into your feelings, if you are able to recognize your own beauty, value, and worth as well as the other person's, then you have managed yourself well and have advanced toward positive behavior.

But if you are accustomed to punishing yourself in the company of other "more attractive" people, you are committing at least one of the cognitive distortions discussed in Chapter 3 (all-or-nothing-thinking, mental filter, and "should" statements), and self-management gets stymied. When you're under serious pressure, you have two choices: you can take the high road or the low road. Taking the high road would mean reminding yourself of what makes you special—like your own beauty, value and worth. Your health, your family, your friends, or your job—so you can stop feeling threatened.

If you aren't able to take the high road yet, you can still balance yourself out by taking emergency measures. Tell yourself whatever it takes to make yourself believe that this other person's life is not perfect. This is a total reality, because no one is perfect. You can tell yourself something like "She looks good, but I bet she has gnarly leg bush," or "Sure, he's built, but I bet he's about as interesting as a penny. . . and has a way smaller penis than me."

I'm encouraging you to do this in *emergencies*—not because I want you to berate other people so you can feel better about yourself, but to show you that sometimes it takes extreme thinking to balance out your own extreme views. If your internal dialogue consists of false and evil things like "I will never be that young or skinny again, so I should stop trying to be happy," or "Only people like that have good lives," or "If I looked like that I wouldn't have any problems," you need to tell yourself something that will take that person down a bunch of notches in your head. When they're off a pedestal and on the same level as the rest of the world, it's a start.

*Note to self: Emergency self-management like this should be used sparingly. Reframing your negative thinking without needing to insult others is the healthier route and a preferable one you will soon achieve. If you make it a habit to put others down to increase your worth, that's excessive defensiveness (and hostile) and not part of getting rad or staying rad. But it's okay to be catty once in a while if it helps you take others off a pedestal.

STAY RAD PRINCIPLE 1—BREATHE.

That's right. The first of these strategies is so easy that all you have to do is exist. Focusing on your breathing is the most basic intervention you can employ to take you out of the emotional part of your brain when you feel distressed, angry, frustrated, down, or insecure, and into the thinking part to regain some emotional control.[2]

Yoga teachers, meditation gurus, and psychologists alike encourage us to relax by breathing through the nose and expanding the belly or chest with air (either work). After that, all you need to do is slowly exhale through your mouth.

Another trick is using the 4:5 rule. When you inhale for the count of four, then exhale for the count of five, you are expending more energy than you are taking in, and your body is put into a relaxed state. I use 4:5, but you should use whatever ratio works best for you. If you are an athlete, yours may be higher than what works for other people (4:7 or 6:9). If you are a senior citizen, you might want to use 2:2 or 2:3 (just in case you're elderly and reading the shit out of this book).

It's all about figuring out what works best for you and trusting it. You don't have to strain yourself. Like I said, whatever helps you to get and stay grounded by exchanging tension for peace..

STAY RAD PRINCIPLE 2—COUNT TO TEN.

How easy is this, right? Counting to ten is another simple thing you can do to practice gaining control of your emotions. If you can do two things at once, like blink and chew at the same time, or talk to your boss and hold in a fart, then guess what? You can count to ten and breathe, too. When you notice yourself feeling any emotion you don't like—such as anger, fear, shame, anxiety, or frustration—you can count to ten and continue breathing, which will stop the production of this emotion long enough to cool down your overheated limbic system and give the rational part of your brain time to catch up.

Since I am pro gentle teaching here, imagine that you and your best friend are running. You happen to be the faster runner, and once you're in the zone, you lose sight of your periphery and only focus on the road ahead. However, at some point you realize your BFF is not close, so you stop and wait for them to catch up. That's what friends do. Let's work to help make your limbic system and your rational brain stay friends, and let's learn to slow the limbic system down so the rational brain can to catch up. The simple act of counting to ten will help.

Use some of that self-awareness you learned in the last chapter to help you notice when a yucko emotion enters the scene. When you notice it's there, count to ten to lessen its blow so you'll be in a better position to make a rational choice about what to say or do next.

STAY RAD PRINCIPLE 3—SMILE AND LAUGH MORE.

Smiling has the power to uplift even the poopiest of moods. Just the physical act, regardless of how genuine, sends signals to your brain that tells it that you're happy. And laughing can be a cathartic experience. It can alleviate a superchunk of the negative energy you feel and lighten your heart. The act of laughing— preferably a genuine larf, but even a "fake it till you make it" one—will help you get better at lightening up, which in turn will make you less prone to developing stress and other shit feelings. Consider laughing an orgasm for your mood. How many people feel pissed after that? Not many.

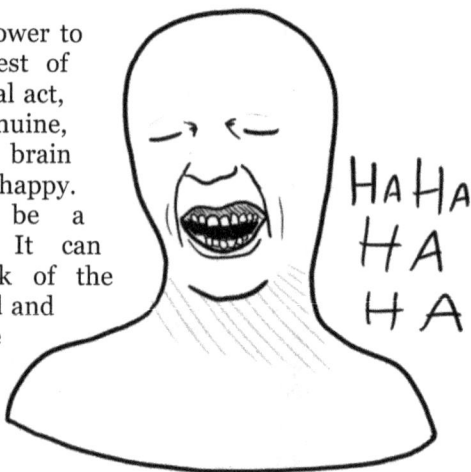

Allowing yourself to smile when you are experiencing a rotten emotion requires you to move out of the feeling state you are in and into a rational one instead. Laughing can set off a chain reaction that coalesces these two magnificent parts of your brain and helps show them that they can in fact become besties forever. When you practice self-management, you are teaching harmonious coexistence to your two states of mind, which promotes optimal health and well-being for the organism at hand—you. Change happens on a physiological level when you move smoothly between the thinking and feeling parts of your brain. It's like building a magical bridge that paves your way to awesomeness. Not to say that you should reflexively crack up at everything that happens to you—just try incorporating more larfs into your daily livin.

STAY RAD PRINCIPLE 4—TAKE CONTROL OF YOUR SELF-TALK.

The average person has approximately 50,000 thoughts per day, according to research.[3] 50,000!!! That is a high number of anything. 50,000 days equals just under 137 years, which is more than any of us will ever live. Over a 24-hour period we take over 20,000 breaths,[4] our heart beats about 100,000 times,[5] and our eyes will blink approximately 15,000 times.[6] The processes that enable all of these activities to take place occur outside of our awareness.

Since thinking is an important process, which we're almost always doing (except when we're asleep, but even then our brains are still doing neat stuff) and we generate 50,000 thoughts throughout the day, it's a good idea for us to learn about what goes into this process. Every time you experience any one of these 50,000 thoughts, your brain produces chemicals that have the ability to trigger reactions, including emotions that you feel throughout your body. Our thoughts occur on a continuum of consciousness. Some puncture our awareness more than others.

Stopping at a red light, changing the radio station, walking—all of these things require thinking, but we are less cognizant of the thoughts that are braided into these experiences than, say, the thought we have of "Holy hell, this bitch is all sorts of crazy" when some cunty person cuts us off while driving.

My point here is that some thoughts move into our consciousness with more force than others, and these will be the easiest to capture because they are the most pronounced. As a simple exercise, scan your day today, or the last week, to identify something that instigated a surge of emotion within you (either positive or negative). The easier it is to identify, the stronger the experience punctured your awareness.

Increasing your level of awareness so you can implement the changes you want in your life, requires you to think in a different way that lets you identify and track the thoughts that are having the most influence on you. This process is sometimes referred to as developing your third eye, and it involves getting in touch with something called your "self-talk."

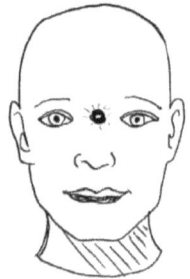

SELF TALK
REFERS TO THE
INTERNAL DIALOGUE WE HAVE
——— WITH ———
OURSELVES

Self-talk refers to the internal dialogue we have with ourselves. Remember the continuum of consciousness? We may not be aware of the messages we're generating and sending to ourselves.

We all have thoughts that communicate something to us. When you get dressed for work or school or whatever it is you get dressed for (rodeo, clown college, Civil War roleplay), you might think, "I look really, really good," or "I look pretty good and totally presentable," or "I look like a dog's stinky ass." These thoughts are sending you a message. Let's take a look at some messages we may be sending ourselves when we have thoughts like this.

> Thought: *"I look really, really good."*
> Message: *I am so cool. I really value the way I look and everyone in the world agrees that I'm the best.*

> Thought: *"I look pretty good and totally presentable."*
> Message: *I like me. I need improvement in some ways, but don't we all?*

> Thought: *"I look like a dog's stinky ass."*
> Messages: *I'm such a loser. I'll never be good-looking, and I should resign myself to a life of shit misery because that's all I deserve.*

Our self-talk delivers the messages that live inside the thoughts we have, and the messages that have the biggest impact are the ones that affect our emotions most, so it will benefit you to start paying attention to them. In order to expose the overt and covert messages you're sending to your consciousness, **you'll need to illuminate the heck out of the thoughts you're having.** What are you feeling, and why is it influencing you the way it is?

HELLO BRAIN! What are my messages today?

YOU ARE APPROACHING THIS BOOK WITH AN OPEN MIND. YOU ARE WILLING TO CHANGE. YOU PLAN TO TAKE CHARGE OF YOUR LIFE.

For example, thinking "I feel sad because I got into an argument with my boyfriend" may lead to self-talk that says, "It's always my fault. I'm the worst girlfriend and he should leave me." The *what* part, the feeling of being sad, is real. But the *why* part, the explanation you gave yourself, is bunk. "It's always my fault" is a dysfunctional and inaccurate statement. If you can spend some time thinking about the messages you send yourself, you are more inclined to notice them in real time so you can challenge them.

you CONTROL WHAT YOU ALLOW YOURSELF to THINK

Another reason it is so important to pick up that telephone and eavesdrop on your psyche is that once you familiarize yourself with your self-talk and are more aware of the messages you are sending yourself, you will realize that you control what you allow yourself to think. Yes, people, you, YoU, YOU, have the power to control the messages you send yourself, which in turn will effect what? The EMOTIONS you feel.

The thoughts we have CREATE OUR REALITY, AND OUR REALITY is CREATED BY THE THOUGHTS we HAVE.

The thoughts we have create our reality, and our reality is created by the thoughts we have.

If you have a disagreement with your partner, are you going to think, "This sucks and it's hopeless," or "This sucks, but we can resolve it and get through this"? The way we experience things is similar (touch a stove, we all get burned; lose a fart in public, we feel embarrassed—well, many of us), but the thoughts and feelings we have about those experiences vary. There is no way around this, and the sooner you realize that the thoughts you allow yourself have a profound influence on you, the easier it will be to learn about yourself and improve at self-management. This, my friend, will help you to not only get awesome, but stay awesome.

STAY RAD PRINCIPLE 5—VISUALIZE YOURSELF BEING SUCCESSFUL.

S-U-C-C-E-S-S, that's the way you spell success!

Next in line is the power of visualization to help transform you into a self-aware, self-managed powerhouse. In order to change your brain—to effect literal, physical change by forming the new neural pathways required to make behaviors stick—one of the things you need to do is see yourself being successful. In other words, you have to envision it and use your imagination to create images of yourself accomplishing the goal or change you are trying to make.

Your brain processes not only what you perceive, but also what you imagine. When you compare MRI brain scans of someone watching a sunset to someone imagining one, the scans are very similar. The same brain regions are stimulated in both instances.[7]

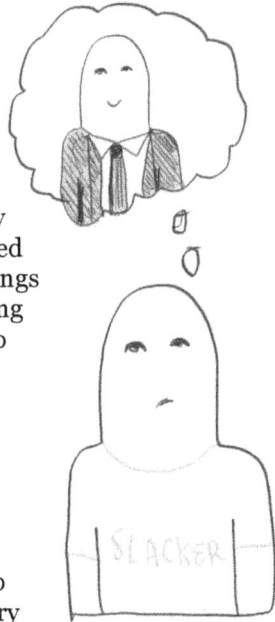

Some people use meditation to improve their visualizing skills, which is great, but isn't your only option. You can visualize whenever your hands are free and no one's life depends on you giving them your attention. So, don't ✗ do this when you're driving, but yes, do it ✓ during a *Game of Thrones* commercial break. Again, don't try this ✗ when you're feeding your kids, but yes, ✓ when you're on the treadmill or elliptical or commode. Another good time is at night, when you're tucked in, so precocious and full of wonderment, when the noise of the day has quieted and you are in a more relaxed state.

Visualization simply means PICTURING YOURSELF SUCCEEDING

Here is what you need to do to visualize: Close your eyes and picture yourself succeeding in situations that are the most difficult for you to manage emotionally. Picture as many details as you can in that beautiful psyche of yours in order to set the perfect scene. Is it your environment at work? At home? At a friend's? A large family gathering? The gym? At school? It all depends on you, what you find most challenging, and what you're trying to change. Imagine as many sensory experiences as you can, meaning the sounds, sights, smells, etc., of the environment where you picture yourself kicking ass. Concentrate until you can mentally transport yourself into the scene. Pay attention to the emotions that get stirred up and identify them as you envision yourself being there. Hold these emotions and acknowledge their presence.

After you've got a good hold on the emotions this scene generates, and you believe you can tolerate and manage them for the time being, *PICTURE YOURSELF* behaving the way *you would like*. *PICTURE YOURSELF* saying the things *you would like*. *PICTURE YOURSELF* controlling the emotions you have and carrying yourself the way *you would like*. Allow yourself to connect to the positive and validating emotions you have when you visualize yourself saying and doing the things you want in this scenario.

> *"Next time I encounter my friend's obnoxious boyfriend with a personality so maddening it makes me burp vomit, I will (1) remind myself that I only have to tolerate him for a short time, (2) focus my attention elsewhere and try my best to ignore him, and (3) sit as far away from him as possible. I will take deep breaths as needed, and leave the situation with a calm mood, low stress level, and head held high. I do not have to let anyone push my buttons because I am in control of my reactions."*

Research has long established that having specific plans increases our chances of success,[8] so practicing it in your head will give you the upper hand when it's go time in real life. Since you can see yourself succeeding, you are more equipped to succeed when you try.

STAY RAD PRINCIPLE 6—TRY TO TAKE SOMETHING POSITIVE AWAY FROM EVERYONE YOU ENCOUNTER.

Uwwww Weeee. This one is hard for a lot of folks, because once our emotions are charged up, it's easy for our feelings to override our rationality. Learning to take something positive away from every encounter you have with people is a challenge, but not impossible, and something to strive for.

Thinking about what makes you most defensive is a good way to start this learning process because when we have a defensive reaction, we are not the most rational. When we're defensive, our emotions can hijack our logic. What gets us feeling defensive can be attributed to any one or a combination of the feelings we all have: happy, sad, angry, afraid, ashamed. Spending time understanding what sets you off will increase your self-management skills.

Interesting to note is that sometimes feeling happy, or even just being around others who seem to be happy, makes some people irritated and defensive. It's not just sadness, anger, fear, and shame that elicit their defensiveness. It could be that they're depressed and don't believe happiness exists, or that they're confused or angered by the idea of happiness because they want it but have never felt it the way they think they should.

Changing your frame of mind to be more receptive to lessons from others is a free tool you can use to improve your well-being. Yes, it's hard, because it's taking something valuable away from the people you encounter—people you might not like, and quite possibly despise. But the truth is, if you can do it, the joke's on them. You're the one in charge and able to respond to your emotions with poise and control. Bradberry and Greaves state, "Approaching everyone you encounter as though they have something valuable to teach you—something that you will benefit from—is the best way to remain flexible, open-minded and much less stressed."9

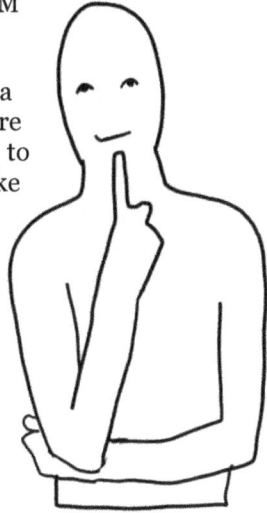

So whether it's the cunty driver that cut you off or the friend's loudmouth boyfriend who has an opinion about everything, take something positive away from them. Driver = be thankful you are not that careless with your life and that this butthole didn't cause an accident. Friend's bigmouth boyfriend = use your encounter with him as an exercise in humility. Oftentimes people with unfounded opinions are experiencing real suffering behind all that ignorance.

If you try to place a positive framework on things and take something valuable away from the encounter, you are less likely to stay upset after you become upset. Feeling upset is not a bad thing, though. Remember, *all your feelings are always okay all of the time.* And believe it or not, sometimes showing displeasure shows that you have self-esteem and value yourself. It shows that there are certain things you don't like, don't appreciate, and are unwilling to tolerate. Getting upset is normal, but staying upset is what you want to prevent.

Conclusion

Working to understand yourself better and gain control of your thoughts and behaviors will help you avoid being hijacked by coked-out emotions. When you're able to do this, you're able to cope with your emotions in healthy ways, manage your thoughts, and command your behavior the way you want to. Next we'll discuss how people change, and identify the processes we all follow when we attempt to do so. Almost to the end, baby. Stay with me.

PART III: CHANGE

Chapter 8 | What happens as we prepare for change

Inspired by failure

My first genuine interest in the process of change began a long time ago when I was an intern in my master's program. I did my training for the year at a residential substance abuse/detox facility and I had the opportunity to work with some great people whose misfortunate it was to battle and suffer from addictions they couldn't seem to beat. I saw a number of these people come in and out through the year, and I was stumped. They ruined their lives, ravaged their bodies, lost their jobs, alienated themselves from their friends and family, and yet they kept using.

Some of them, that is. Some of them kicked it, worked the program, and stayed clean, while others were not able to. What was different between the ones who stayed clean and the ones who continued to relapse?

The explanation for why some people never get clean and sober and others are successful at completing detox after 0, 3, 8, 14, 25, and even 79 relapses is multifaceted. But (and this is a big but) while there are a bunch of layers to this issue, there is also order, because research has shown that the stages of change follow a progression. Someone who continues to fail at something they are trying to change is either getting stuck or has passively resigned. Getting stuck is sometimes a part of the process, but staying stuck is a total bummer, sucks nard, and stifles your efforts.

The great news is that the stages of change can be applied to just about any situation. What do you want to change in your life most? Exercise more? Lose weight? Eat better? Be more social? Be less aggro? Be a better partner to your mate? Be nicer to your mom and dad? Be a better employee? Change your occupation? Go back to school? Whatever it is, you hold the power to generate changes in your life. Knowledge is power, so before we identify the six stages of change we must first understand some of the things that happen as human beings change.

The nine processes that facilitate and support change

As we change, a variety of processes are working on a cellular level within us, but the ones we will address here are the most powerful.[1] As we go through them, think of times when you've practiced each of them. I'm sure if you look hard enough, you can find an example. My hope is that these explanations will help you label some of the awesome things you're already doing. My double hope is that learning about these nine processes will make you want to practice them more, because the more you practice, the easier it gets.

#1—Consciousness-raising

You know the **"Aha!"** moments that Oprah talked about all the time? The thing that happens when your stars align and you have an amazing moment of clarity about something? That's the basic idea behind consciousness-raising.

Consciousness-raising is a fundamental part of all major therapies because it helps people become more self-aware, which is a major precursor to growth. Carl Jung once said, "Until you make the unconscious conscious, it will direct your life and you will call it fate." Any time you increase the knowledge that is available to you, you are raising your consciousness and gaining more understanding and control of your life. This is one of the things a good therapist would try to help you do.

Having consciousness-raising experiences is important because they can leave a lasting impression on your life and compel you to make a change. Getting to experience this first hand is amazing, and helping others do it is also incredibly meaningful. It's one of the many perks in my field, and I try very hard to help my clients have these moments. Sometimes when folks realize *why* they do certain things, exposing the roots of their behavior, they gain an understanding so strong that it moves them to change.

Examples include the woman who learned to be more assertive after realizing it was difficult for her to say no to people because her mother taught her women should put other people's needs first—which is untrue.

Or the young man who reduced his alcohol consumption after recognizing that his motive for drinking wasn't because he liked the taste, but because it helped him feel more comfortable in his own skin. Or the serial dater who stopped rushing into relationships after she came to understand that she breaks up with partners when she feels like she's getting too close because she is afraid they will eventually leave her, and this makes her feel vulnerable.

Exercise

Now, think of your own consciousness-raising experience. Identify something that happened in your life that **shot a lightning bolt straight to your consciousness** and made you have a realization so powerful that it changed the way you see things.

#2—Emotional arousal

Emotional arousal is what happens when you experience emotion on a level so grand, so intense and so strong it compels you to make a change. It is related to consciousness-raising, but works on a deeper level because it involves the evocation of poignant emotions. It's sometimes called a cathartic experience, and it's a super powerful thing—think the combined force that Batman, Ironman, Superman, Spiderman, Megaman, and Redman would have.

For example, watching videos about factory farming could change the way you feel about eating meat. The footage you find after a Google search of "factory farming videos" might leave you feeling demoralized, but it may also serve as a vehicle for change. Certain sights, explanations, and feedback have the power to generate commanding emotions that instigate real change in our behavior. (Also, if you are a meat eater, please consider buying grass-fed and pastured meats from farmers who employ humane and sustainable practices. Check out http://www.eatwild.com/ for more information. "Ingest the best" is a good motto to have when nourishing your body and mind.)

Other examples of emotional arousal occur from real life tragedies. If someone you love is dying of lung cancer, and while lying on their deathbed they ask you to give up smoking, you might be inclined to do so. If your doctor informs you that both arteries in your heart are 95% blocked, you might opt for a salad and steer clear of the big beef and cheddar. Drastic things like this often compel us to change. Psychodrama in movies, music videos, and other types of media can also elicit these deafening emotions that initiate change.

Whether or not the change becomes permanent will vary, but it is certain the energy that can be created through these channels has the power to move you. How many dudes started working out super hard after they saw *Fight Club, Bronson,* or *300*, right?!

#3—Self-reevaluation

Self-reevaluation is another part of the change process, and it necessitates that you assess your problem in an honest and genuine way. Meaning, you step out of denial and stop bullshitting yourself.

It also means that you visualize yourself succeeding and let yourself imagine what your life would look like if you were able to overcome the dang issue that is bringing you down. The end result of successful self-reevaluation is that you believe and feel certain that your life would be better if you were able to change and resolve the issue at hand.

When applying self-reevaluation, people often weigh the pros and cons of changing a specific behavior, and they spend quality time reflecting upon the ways their lives would be different if they were able to change.

The process of self-reevaluation allows us to see how our behavior conflicts with our personal values. If you often act like a Turd Ferguson to your partner but don't like how snapping at him or her makes you feel, after self-reevaluation you may be inclined to get your behavior and personal values more aligned.

If you're trying to lose weight but still have poor eating habits, you may re-eval your behavior so that you are more inclined to resist late-night treats from that nasty little sugar temptress. When done with authenticity, self-reevaluation reinforces our motivation and gives us the **extra kick in the ass** we need to start a behavior change.

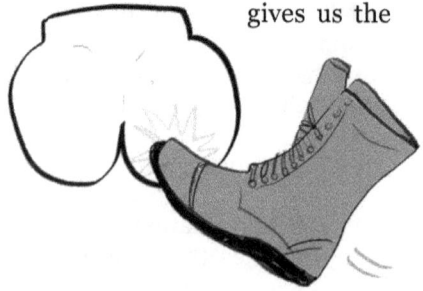

Exercise

Try some self-reevaluation now. Say this to yourself and let it resonate:

I know no one is perfect and that we are all works in progress, but at the end of the day, my life matters. I am important and I can be happier and better if I really try to change.

The thing I really need to change about my life right now is

_____

When I am able to successfully change this, here are some of the pros & cons:

_____

I will feel

_____

when I put in the work to achieve the results I want.

#4—Commitment

Commitment is another significant part of the change process. This word with its three little syllables is SOOOOO important, because when you make a true commitment to change, you are accepting responsibility for your actions. It requires you to get your feet out of the huge pile of denial doo-doo and step onto a much cleaner and stronger platform.

Part of commitment is accepting responsibility. This is a sign of maturity and strength. It doesn't mean you have to be perfect and that you can't make mistakes along your journey, because that's not possible. You will make some mistakes. That is normal, acceptable, and okay. Accepting responsibility means acknowledging that you are the only one who can think, act, and speak for yourself, and that you are accountable for the changes you see or don't see.

It is critical that you don't throw in the towel after a slip-up or goof, because committing and recommitting are part of the change process. Commitment only takes two steps! The first is telling yourself that you are choosing to make a change. This is where you mentally prep yourself, and then all of the magical light bulbs in your pretty head light up and encourage you to commit.

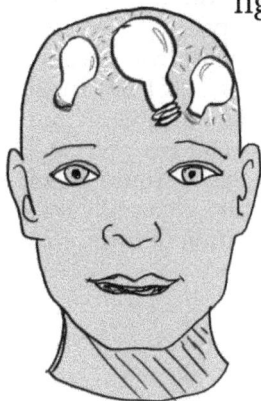

The second step is going public and telling other people that you have decided to make your change. Public commitments can be more powerful than private ones because they invite elevated pressure. The shame or guilt that comes if you are unsuccessful with sticking to your change is more hefty if the audience is bigger.

If you're the only one who knows you tried and failed, it may be easier to handle, as opposed to 10, 200, or 1000 of your FB friends, IG or Twitter followers that keep up with yo bidnass.

You have to be careful with this. Sometimes a public announcement is used in hopes that it alone will compel you to actualize the change you want. If you make public announcements before you are truly ready to commit, you could get wrapped up in a shit storm of guilt and shame due to repetitive failures. Don't use an audience as your main catalyst to change. This is something that first has to happen within yourself. Use other peeps as a way to help you stay honest and accountable.

Exercise

Have you ever used other people to help you reach a goal or make a change? Think of an example, then fill in the blank.

I remember when I asked _____

to help me with _____.

#5—Environmental control

You gain environmental control when you restructure your environment to suit the new way of being which you've committed to.

Common examples include people who get rid of candy, ice cream, and processed foods when they are trying to eat less sugar. Or putting up motivational signs by your mirror, such as "I am totally rad and I can achieve my goals," or "If I fall I will pick my sweet ass right back up," or "I will be patient and accepting of myself, because growth takes time and is a process," in an effort to increase self-esteem. A final example would be an individual in recovery deciding to take a different route home to avoid seeing his old liquor shop until his temptation to drink was no longer a threat.

Exercise

Think of at least one example of where you modified your environment so you would be more inclined to achieve the desired success.

Thinking Space

#6—Countering

Countering, or counter-conditioning, is the part of change where you cut out an unhealthy response and replace it with a healthy one. This requires you to **identify a toxic thought or behavior and exchange it for something nontoxic.** It's a basic way of realizing that you don't like something and that you have the power to do something about it.

Eating an apple with some Nutella on it when your sweet tooth is hootin and hollerin in place of five pieces of cake or half a tray of brownies would be an example. Another example is deciding to go for a walk after you get into an argument, instead of losing your temper and calling everyone flaming bags of dickballs from hell. Or taking a hot shower after a stressful day as a way of unwinding, instead of downing a fifth of Jack right when you get home. Or training yourself to take a breath when you have a negative and dispiriting thought like "I'm a loser going nowhere," so you can then reframe it to "I'm feeling down, but I have options and can make a change."

By replacing an unhealthy thought or action with a healthier one, you are setting yourself up for success the next time you have an urge to go against what you vowed to change. Cue fireworks here, because this is significant:

SPENDING TIME FINDING OUT the COUNTERING ACTIVITIES THAT WORK BEST FOR YOU IS KEY.

If you're trying to be healthier, giving up Diet Coke and replacing it with Diet Pepsi or switching from calling everyone buttlicks to dickholes when you're peeved is not gonna do it. You have to find something more meaningful.

Exercise

Right now, think about an instance of actual, successful change and what you countered that behavior with. Now think of something that you want to change, and what might work to counter it.

Thinking Space

#7—Rewards

The effectiveness of countering depends on rewarding yourself, which is something you already understand because we discussed it in Chapter 4. This is an important part of the change process, because if you experience a reward after a particular behavior, you are more inclined to repeat it in the future. If we can train ourselves to experience a reward after we counter an unhealthy behavior, we will be more likely to behave that way in the future—and have an easier time doing it.

Training in this sense is just a matter of helping you illuminate positive aspects of your modified behavior. It can be reminding yourself how much better you breathe without cigarettes, how much more money you have without all that drinking, how much looser your clothes are without stuffing all those Ho Hos into your gullet, and how improved is your relationship with your family now that your rage'ahol is managed.

Praising yourself is a simple and constructive way to reward yourself. It involves acknowledging the positive things that have come about as a direct result of your efforts to change. Some people have a super hard time letting themselves take pride in their successes. If this sounds like you, you need to learn how to accept personal accolades. Start by just acknowledging that you—like the whole lot of us—are capable of doing good things.

If you have been successful at changing something that didn't serve you well, then let that goodness rain down on you because you (You! You!! You!!!) earned it.

The fact is, you *are* good enough and you need to experience what self-made success feels like.

Rewards other than self-praise include buying yourself something or treating yourself to an extraordinary special gift once you have achieved the change on which you've worked so hard.

Exercise

What rewards do you give yourself? Vacations? DVDs? Clothes? Shoes? Fancy dinners? Art? If you can't identify at least one, you need to hypothesize right now about what a feasible reward to a behavior you change would look like.

Making it feasible is important, because if you don't have extra money, when you finally quit smoking, you may not be able to buy that original Mark Penxa painting just yet (but soon you will). We have to be realistic with our rewards, and I'm trusting that you have the insight to implement this. Another example: say you have eighty pounds to lose and you reward yourself with a trip around the world after you're five pounds down, you may be indulging in premature action. Be reasonable here, but make sure you give yourself the acknowledgment you deserve along the way.

#8—Cultivate helping relationships

Cultivating helping relationships (relationships that heal pain) is another part of the change process. It's proven that enlisting social support has multiple benefits during times of distress, and when you're trying to change, it's no different. Yes, the process of change is a very personal one, but it doesn't mean others can't help you out along your way.

The truth is,

CHANGING
CAN BE A
MOTHERFUCKER

It's hard work and sometimes—in fact, oftentimes—talking with someone who cares about you can ease your burden and reinforce your capabilities. It's one reason my entire field of clinical psychology exists. People need someone to talk to, and they need someone to bear witness as they release some of the stress, frustration, sadness, anger, fear, pain, shame, and trauma they hold onto.

Exercise

Riddle me this: Who do you turn to first when you're in despair?

#9—Social liberation

The last little station of our nine processes refers to an external force known as social liberation. It's not necessarily anything you do; rather, it incorporates any alternative that your public environment can provide to assist in your process of change.

Twenty-four-hour gyms are a good example of this, as well as restaurants that offer options for various dietary preferences. These things may serve to facilitate change within you because they are empowering. Being able to work out anytime you want to is convenient, and could reinforce your motivation to follow through. Having options besides a puny piece of celery with ketchup when you dine out may reinforce your willingness to stick with your diet. On a grander level, Alcoholics Anonymous and other support groups are some of the most socially liberating forces out there. Anything in the public realm that creates opportunities for you to realize the change you want represents social liberation.

Exercise

Can you identify one example of how social liberation has helped you make a positive change?

REVIEW of the nine major precursors to change

1.) Consciousness-raising—increasing your level of awareness

2.) Emotional arousal—emotion so powerful it compels you to change

3.) Self-reevaluation—calling yourself out and visualizing success

4.) Commitment—accepting responsibility, trying and retrying until you get results

5.) Environmental control—restructuring your environment

6.) Countering—out with the old habits, in with the new behaviors

7.) Rewards—letting yourself feel good after you make a change

8.) Cultivating helping relationships—seeking support from those who care

9.) Social liberation—taking advantage of parts of your environment that reinforce change

You have the ability to make the changes you want. You have done it in the past, and you can do it again now.

Chapter 9 | What happens as we change

"At certain moments in history, there are individuals whose minds are prepared to recognize the importance of things that unprepared minds ignore or throw away"[1]

The six stages of change

At any given moment, there are forces in your life available to help you become the person you want to be. The tricky part is recognizing those forces and letting them do their thing. In this chapter, we'll talk about change, and how you have the power to metamorphose and live the life you want. It's true, it's amazing, and it's an integral part of getting and staying rad. The reason this is so damn mind-blowing is that it proves there is always hope. Even if a behavior has had consistent reinforcement for years and years and years, it is not set in stone, and people can in fact change.

The progression goes something like this:

Change your thinking→change your brain→change your

behavior→change your *Life*

The six stages of change I outline next are known to be the progression that successful changers follow.[2] Men, women, young, old, rich, not so rich, smart, less smart, etc., all of us follow this projection as we change. If you're going to be successful, you must meet the objectives of each stage, which takes time and commitment. As we move on, remember two things:

1.) Change, t'aint always easy. Along our journey to Mount Awesomeness, it's possible to have a breakdown and get stuck.

2.) Completing one stage does not automatically get you to the next one.

Setting realistic goals is also a must. If you try to accomplish something for which you are not equipped, you set yourself up for an epic fail. I encourage you to start with something small or miniature, and after you achieve that success—and reward yourself for it, maybe in the form of a self-esteem boost, feelings of validation, happiness, or pride, or a reasonable purchase— then go bigger. Start with a Mini-Cooper-sized issue before you set out for an eighteen-wheeler-Mack-sized one. If you start small and succeed, you'll be ready to tread valiantly ahead and keep on keepin on. So chin up, baby! Bite off just as much as you can chew.

Stage 1: Precontemplation

Denial and resistance mark the precomtemplation stage. "What problem? I don't have a problem. You have a problem. Just because I haven't left the house in ten days, have stopped talking to my friends, and have a panic attack when my phone rings, does not mean I have an issue."

Even though your family, friends, coworkers, neighbors, pets, carpet, countertops, and walls can see the problem, you're not allowing yourself to acknowledge it. People in this stage have no usual intention of changing—instead, they want to change the people around them.

People who are closed off to information about their problems prevent consciousness-raising (the first process of change), and they shun any attempt to counter their "ignorance is bliss" attitude. They attribute their issue to genetics, family, society, or the biggest catchall of them all, which can't even defend itself, destiny. They pass the buck and the responsibility to an external force they cannot control.

Lord knows, I've been there. Before I stopped smoking I convinced myself that I was going to be in the George Burns category when I kicked the bucket, not the "cancer ate my throat before I turned forty" one. So I'm not preaching here, I'm just saying that

WHEN WE FORFEIT RESPONSIBILITY WE ARE IN FOR TROUBLE.

Pitfall 1: Demoralization

Demoralization is a significant part of this stage. People who are stuck here think their situation is hopeless, so they adopt a "Fuck it, I'm gonna keep doing what I've been doing" attitude. We've all been here, and we've all known someone in this stage. Feeling hopeless is a normal feeling to have sometimes, but if you don't manage it, it can take control of (and poison) your thinking and your behavior. Our emotions are associated with our thoughts, so disproving a negative thought that is false and stymies your success is important here.

Telling yourself something as simple as "I feel like nothing in the world will help me, but I know that can't be true. I am capable of change just like everyone else is" can be a good start.

When someone buys into the "It's hopeless and I can't do anything about it" mentality, it's both soul-crushing and kind of pathetic. I know "pathetic" may be a strong word here, but seriously, when you resign your free will, you're acting like a butt. Free will, i.e., the ability to make active choices, is part of what makes us human and something to be revered—not taken for granted.

Precontemplation is a natural part of the change process, but I want to make sure your fine little booty doesn't get stuck there. Spending your life in this stage blows hard, and you deserve better.

At the same time, you have to remember that you get what you put into things. If you want to get the most out of yourself, the situation requires brutal honesty. Strip away your defenses and take a close look at yourself.

Pitfall 2: Putting up defenses

The common defenses seen in this stage are denial, projection, displacement and rationalization. If you notice yourself ignoring other people's concerns about you, or becoming super angry or touchy when someone brings up your behavior, then take a look-see at whether or not you tend to be a precontemplator. We've all been there. We've all gone there. And we'll all still go there sometimes. No one is judging you, so just be honest with yourself and cop to it.

Stage 2: Contemplation

In the second stage of change, people acknowledge that they need to change, and they can even envision what it will take to get there, but the resistance to do it is still present. Guys and gals in contemplation mode are ambivalent at this point, which means they're open to learning, reading, and talking about their problem, but still opposed to action.

People are not prepared for action until they gain a greater understanding of their behavior through consciousness-raising. The tricky-dicky thing here is that

The BREADTH of
UNDERSTANDING
A PERSON NEEDS
VARIES

and getting caught up on needing more and more and MORE information can be a rrrrrreally great stall tactic.

Ever hear of "paralysis through analysis?" That's what I mean. That you're almost ready, but you keep convincing yourself that you need just a little more this or a little more that before you'll be ready to make the change. The end result is that you'll keep spinning your wheels and get nowhere. *I'll make this change after I do more research on it. After my workload lightens up. After I finish organizing my den. After my mom visits. After Flag Day 2020. After, after, after.*

There's always an after, but there's no time like the present. You have to seize the day to make progress.

Aside from wanting absolute certainty and to possess all the information that exists about your particular issue, there are three common traps that prevent people from moving out of the contemplation stage: waiting for the magic moment, wishful thinking, and premature action.

Stalling tactic 1: Waiting for the magic moment

The magic moment is not when you boink your girlfriend or boyfriend for the first time. This pitfall happens when you adhere to some sort of mystical belief that someday, somehow, in some way, everything in your life will align and then, and only then, making the change you want will be possible.

If you or someone you know has talked about the same annoying, punishing, nauseating topic for an exasperating long time and still makes no change even though he or she knows what needs to be done, they may be waiting for this magic moment. **NEWS FLASH** —this is your way of stalling.

Stalling tactic 2: Wishful thinking

Wishful thinking is common among those lovely folks who want to dream away their problems. They wish they could eat a tub of ice cream and not gain weight, wish they could be a size medium without exercising, wish they could drink as much as they want without losing control, wish they could get a better job without going out to look for one, or wish they could have better relationships without working on them. This passive approach is not conducive to success.

NEWS FLASH —ain't no Kazaam genie gonna come out of a bottle to help you.

Stalling tactic 3: Premature action

Premature action is similar to announcing things to the world before you have made a full commitment to change. This is popular among people who are compelled to change because of pressure or ultimatums from family or friends. How far do you think you can get when your primary motivation is an attempt to appease someone else? Not far at all.

The payoff for action—albeit premature action—is that it can alleviate some of the guilt and social pressure you feel. After you try and fail, you can tell others to go suck an egg, and like the mudguards on all trucks south of the airport, say, "Back Off."

Trying something before you've reached an authentic commitment to it implants the erroneous notion in your head that you honestly tried and genuinely failed and you can now get back to doing what you were doing because it's hopeless. If you are not invested in the actions you take, and if they are not born out of the depths of your own personal wants, desires, and needs, then you're going to fall short and be unsuccessful.

NEWS FLASH —You (you, you, you, you, you, you) must want the change you seek.

Spending time in the contemplation stage is a natural, normal, acceptable, and appropriate part of your process, but staying there is not. Stalling out is a coping mechanism because it keeps you comfortable and safe in your world. While this protective measure is a good thing in theory (it's your psyche's way of protecting you), you don't need it now. People fear change, but change is inevitable. Growth is optional.

Leaving your comfort zone takes courage, But it's necessary if you want bona fide change.

If you can do it, the end of the contemplation stage is marked by feelings of anxiety, excitement, anticipation, and activity.

Stage 3: Preparation

People who make it to this stage have released themselves from contemplation's jaws and are now planning to initiate a change within the very next month. They prepare for the change by making adjustments to their life and their environment. Their ambivalence has not reached full resolution, but their willingness and desire to take action overpower it.

Awareness in this stage is heightened and the anticipation is palpable. Think Ferris Bueller right before his parents got home at the end of the day—that's palpable. People in this stage may have already begun making small behavioral changes, such as cutting down on cigarettes, increasing physical activity by taking the stairs instead of an elevator whenever possible, or more often initiating emotionally laden conversations with their mate in an attempt to get closer.

In this stage, you use the processes of self-reevaluation and commitment to prepare for action. You take small steps, set a date for beginning the change, create a plan of action, and maybe even decide to tell others about it.

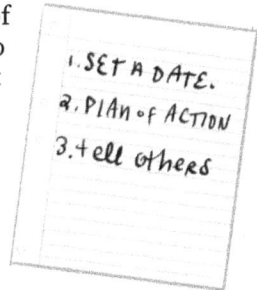

1. SET A DATE.
2. PLAN OF ACTION
3. tell others

Hazard warning #1: Cold turkey? More like stinkin bologna

People who attempt to cut out a behavior cold turkey limit their chances of success. Change that sticks and has long-lasting results happens after careful planning (precontemplation and contemplation), and with a solid plan (preparation).

Hazard warning #2: Expect anxiety

Like it or not, anxiety is a passenger on this journey, and whether it was invited, hitch-hiked, or grifted its dang way onboard, it's going with you. If you can remember what you learned in Chapter 4, you will recall the value of accepting your anxiety and will therefore not coil into the fetal position when you feel it.

Hazard warning #3: Accept failure

Be aware that your attempt at action may fail, despite your rock-solid plan and your genuine commitment. Accept that this is okay. Tell yourself that if you try and fail, you will pick yourself up again, because it's only a failure if you don't learn anything from it.

IF YOU TRY AND FAIL AND LEARN SOMETHING, IT BECOMES A LESSON.

As you embark on your voyage of change, tell yourself that you will put forth the most heroic effort you can and if you fail, which isn't your intention, you will be stronger, better, and closer to your goal for having tried.

Also, let yourself experience a reward for your willingness to try, so that your behavior will be reinforced and you will be inclined to keep on trying until you nail that behavior to the wall and make it say uncle. As we have already established, you are more likely to repeat a behavior that yields a positive outcome than a behavior that yields a negative one.

The way you frame things in your mind influences how you interpret an event, and how you interpret it will shape your experience. In this sense, you are your biggest problem, but you're also your very own solution. Try your very best, and if your best is unsuccessful, still frame it as a positive step in the right direction.

So what if you're not seeing all the weight-loss results you want right now, or that you applied to ten jobs and only got one callback, or that the academic program you had your heart set on rejected you, or that the guy you like told you he wasn't interested? So what? Are you going to be devastated and throw all your hard work and awesomeness out the window? You will lose weight if you exercise and stick to eating healthy. If you applied to ten jobs and got one callback, apply to fifty and see what happens, or talk to a professional and get help with your résumé and interviewing skills. The school you had in mind wasn't interested; okay, next? Move on. They're not the only institution in the world offering the program you want. And if they are, study a bit more and retake the admissions test next year. That guy you thought was cute blew you off, so I guess it means he's not worth your time, and he did you a solid by being honest.

See how the way we interpret events can influence our feelings?

Being able to reframe your thinking will make or break you at this stage. When you try something—when you pour your every ounce of wholehearted effort into something—and it doesn't go your way, you need to be able to view it as a success. You have to acknowledge that you tried, so even if you didn't get the results you hoped for, it doesn't mean your efforts were for naught. You did a great thing by trying, so don't stop.

COMMITTING and RECOMMITTING UNTIL YOU REACH YOUR GOAL MAKES IT MUCH MORE LIKELY THAT YOU WILL SUCCEED

Stage 4: Action

Before we go on, I'm going to ask that you take at least one deep breath to center yourself. I'm not there watching you, so I don't know if you'll do it or not, but please just take one (4:5 rule, remember).

If you did, guess what happened? Not only did you demonstrate your cooperative attitude, but you also took action. So now you know you have the capacity to do this in other areas of your life.

Action is an important part of the change process, because it's the culmination of all the wonderful bursts of momentum you set in motion. Think of the coolest clubhouse ever, where the work you did in the precontemplation, contemplation, and preparation stages all meet up and unite forces—like a brain Voltron. The result is action, and action wants to turn everything up to 11. This baby is a real doozy, but in a good way!

Without ACTION you never CHANGE, and without CHANGE you NEVER GROW.

During the action stage of typical change, which lasts for several months, individuals alter their behaviors and modify their surroundings in an overt fashion. This period keeps you very busy physically, because it necessitates that you act, which in and of itself requires movement. This stage requires a great deal of time, commitment, and energy. It is the stage where change is most evident because behaviors are often explicit.

A person in AA may refuse a drink or pass on a gathering altogether because others may be drinking. An individual trying to get in shape embraces the habit of taking walks after dinner and begins lifting weights. A boyfriend who promises to be more loving incorporates more actual hugs, compliments, and endearing sentiments in his day-to-day life with his girlfriend. The little workaholic in cubicle B who knows he's long overdue for a raise at last asserts himself to his supervisor. All of these things have been building within the person, and all of these things require action if they are going to be realized.

While action is a biggy in the change process, don't underestimate all the work that goes into the stages prior to this. Recognizing action as the only way people change is a faulty way of looking at it—you're not seeing the big picture if that's all you focus on. Some people overlook the less-obvious steps that led up to this point.

As you go through the stages of precontemplation, contemplation, and preparation, you are in fact taking action. Altering your thoughts, frame of mind, and emotions, and making all those attempts to commit and recommit, all require action. So even though the first three stages may be more clandestine experiences, they require just as much strength and vigor as the action stage does.

Taking action is rewarding

Sometimes people feel empowered during this stage because it's where all their sacrifices and hard work begin to pay off. It's where you pass go and finally get to collect $200. Where you begin to reap some of the goodness from the little seedlings you sowed in the first three stages, and where your patient efforts begin to take shape.

Being able to see the results of something you've worked so hard to set in motion is validating and can inspire you to continue this behavioral change. Allowing yourself to experience a reward, in the form of positive emotions like pride, joy, increased self-esteem, validation, and excitement reinforces your motivation, which increases the probability of your success. So find positive ways to reward the action you're taking.

Sometimes taking action helps us realize that we do have control over many things in our environment. Acknowledging that you have the power to make a change that helps you become the person you want to be can leave you feeling enlivened and energized. Action compels us into movement, and sometimes that movement is all it takes to give us the energy we need for successful change.

Stage 5: Maintenance

The maintenance stage of change is a nurturing process that requires you to pay attention to the changes you made and sort of look after them as a mother would her child. During this phase, you do whatever you can to preserve the changes you set in motion, so you can uphold the success you've achieved.

Because change doesn't stop with action, your effort and commitment are just as important here as they were in the other four stages. So just as you wouldn't abandon a baby after you cleaned its mud butt and changed its diaper, you wouldn't abandon your efforts once you started to see some results.

It's believed that the maintenance stage can last anywhere between six months and a lifetime, depending on the issue and your level of mastery over it. Without a strong commitment to maintenance there is sure to be relapse, which smacks you back to the precontemplation or contemplation stage.

One of the most important parts of maintenance is countering—which, as you'll recall from Chapter 8, is the process of learning how to replace your problem behavior with a healthier alternative. It takes countering on your part, so it captures the essence of action. Every time you behave in a new way that is more conducive to your well-being and growth, you are taking action that will bring you closer to your ultimate goals.

Passing up a date from someone who treats you like crud because you have decided not to settle, or choosing to drink more water and less moonshine, or refusing a cigarette to maintain your commitment to quitting, would all be examples of behavior change that facilitates your personal growth.

Maintenance requires you to monitor yourself with a
hypervigilant set of eyeballs

until you have mastered the issue you are trying to change. You'll
soon find that as mastery goes up, vulnerability and
susceptibility to relapse go down. Relapses are setbacks you
experience as you attempt to change any unhealthy behavior
you're working on, not only behaviors that are addictive in
nature. Some slip-ups are to be expected and below are the three
risks voted most likely to cause a relapse in their high school
mock elections.

Relapse risk 1: Overconfidence

This happens when a person underestimates the gravity of
their situation. They may diminish the concerns of others while
foolishly inflating their own self-assurance. (Some denial is
present here.) Confidence itself is not a bad thing, but
overconfidence and defensiveness toward people who care about
you will set you back in the long run.

An example would be a person with a twenty-year history of
alcoholism earning thirty days of sobriety and celebrating by
going to a bar for a nonalcoholic beverage. You don't need a bar
to have a water or iced tea, and you may be setting yourself up
for failure.

Relapse risk 2: Daily temptation

Exposing yourself to daily temptation means being around
people, situations, or stimuli that entice you into old ways of
being. It's hanging around situations that make you vulnerable
and have the power to trigger habits you've worked hard to
extinguish.

Ex-smokers who keep ashtrays, lighters, and a half-full "in
case of emergency" pack at home are one example. Another

example is the dieter who buys a bunch of junk food "in case company comes over." Or if a knucklehead used a lonesome gal for a quickie, yet she doesn't delete his phone number.. Or a former drug abuser, continuing to spend time in the same seedy places with the same seedy people. Environmental triggers would be running amok in these scenarios, making everyone more prone to relapsing.

Relapse risk 3: Self-blame

Self-blame is when we punish, berate, demean, and criticize ourselves. How good is that? Think of what being exposed to a degrading environment does to a child. Would it nurture or impede their sense of worth? Even though we're not kids anymore, the messages we're sending ourselves may be having the same destructive effects that a verbally and emotionally abused child would suffer.

I used to tell folks that self-debasement does not accomplish anything, but I stopped saying that. The truth is, it does accomplish something: it sets you back, way back, and it promotes low self-esteem and low self-worth, which both make you susceptible to falling into old patterns, and negative ways of thinking and behaving. So be on the lookout for the self-blame snake, and when it comes around, don't hesitate to drop an anvil, Looney Toons style, right on its head.

Reject your success at your own peril

During the maintenance stage, accepting your successes is a good thing. Some people have a hard time with this, and hold the mistaken belief that an external force such as the support of others, a therapist, a book, God, etc., is the only reason they were able to achieve any positive results. Indeed, there are people and external factors that have had a positive influence on you and helped to facilitate your growth, but the most influential player in the process of change is you.

If you are unable to recognize that you are the only true catalyst for change in your life, then you may be detached from your growth. You have to realize that you are allowing these factors and forces to influence you in a positive way, and you are the one making the changes happen (or not happen) for yourself.

YOU HAVE TO BELIEVE that YOU ARE the DRIVING FORCE IN ORDER TO TRULY CONNECT to your CHANGE

Attributing your success to someone or something else is dangerous, because it leaves the responsibility—for better or worse—on someone else's shoulders. This is a protective and defensive act in that someone who hands off responsibility is, in essence, saying, "Well, if I succeed it's because of you, so if I fail it's because of you too, and I don't have to accept the responsibility for it."

Giving others the credit for your hard work can also be indicative of low self-esteem. Someone who is unable to acknowledge that they caused a successful change may believe, "Well, this change is a good thing, but there is no way I could have done it without the help of X, Y, and Z. They are the real reason I could change." There may be contributing factors to your process of change, but you have to own the fact that you're the *Big Lebowski* here. You let them influence you. If your change is going to be meaningful and if it is going to stick, you must accept responsibility for both your successes and your slip-ups.

That's the way it goes my friend, so when you succeed and become a badass, it's on you. And when you blow it and goof, getting back on track is on you as well. Be warmed by those who line your path along the way, but make damn sure you know that you're the one holding the torch.

Stage 6: Termination

Ahhhh, termination. The final frontier. Think of an example of something in life you have terminated: a habit, a girlfriend or boyfriend, an Ike's sandwich in SF, wearing Hammer pants... the list is yours to complete. By definition, termination refers to the end of something, so it's not hard to guess what it means in this context either.

In this last stage of change, the problem, behavior, or addiction you were trying to overcome no longer represents a threat to you. Its potential to return has ended, and you've pretty much terminated its power, hold, and existence. Part of this happens on an unconscious level and the other on a very conscious one. Let's take a look.

Unconscious termination

The unconscious part is that once you master something, you do all sorts of things you're not even aware of to maintain it. Once a new behavior is established and the old habit is terminated, perpetuating your new way of doing things becomes rote and normalized.

Take Alex, who has adhered to a clean diet and lifestyle for the last four years. When he goes grocery shopping, going down the sugar, bread, cereal, chips, and candy aisles simply does not occur to him. It just doesn't. He has no cravings for those foods because they have been removed from his life for the last 1,460+ days. There is no need for him to pay attention to those aisles, and he doesn't.

Another example deals with that cold-hearted butthead or succubus that broke your heart that one time. If you ever had a hard breakup and never thought you'd get over the other person, and you have gotten over him or her, as in you're to the point where you haven't even thought of their homely little mug until I just brought it up, then hazzah, it's another successful behavior change. It's science yo! They are no longer in your consciousness on a regular basis because you've been successful at terminating your emotional, physical, and psychological connection to them and have moved on.

Conscious termination

Now the other part of termination happens on a conscious level, where you experience a sense of confidence and are assured that the old habit, behavior, or problem will not return. You live your life without fear that you will relapse, and sustaining the change has gotten to the point where it's effortless. It's no longer work anymore. You've paid your dues, cashed everything in at the bank, and are taking this flight to paradise without ever being compelled to look back. If you can get to this point, it's time to take a bow and get out of the ring of fire, AKA the cycle of change, because you've won. Congrats, brah! High five, thumbs up, and a huge hug from me.

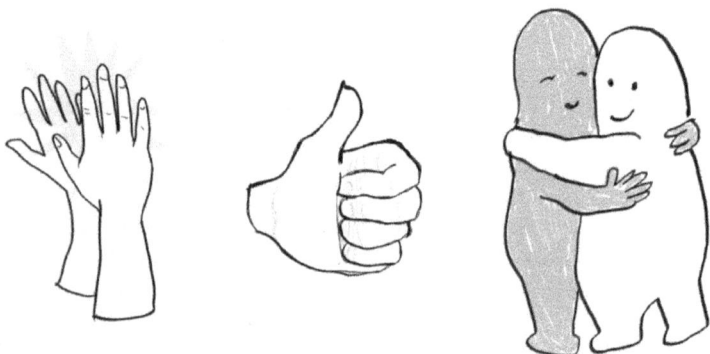

Can all problems be terminated?

There is some debate among nerdlingers like me about whether certain problems are ever truly terminated or are instead kept at a distance through a life of maintenance. As one masters the new and healthy behavior, the maintenance that keeps the old, negative behavior at bay becomes significantly less daunting, but is still required.

There's a difference between someone who doesn't even remember they used to smoke twenty years ago, even when they are around smokers, and someone who quit twenty years ago but still devises a plan of action in case they're tempted to have a cigarette at a party. The first person has overcome his or her addiction to the point where the temptation to relapse is nonexistent. The latter is a person who is smart about their triggers, and has planned in accordance. Both are in a good place, but one's temptations are nonexistent and the other's are very present.

Everyone can make successful changes to their behavior, but some of us are going to need to work at it indefinitely.

REVIEW

The six stages of change:

1.) Precontemplation—*I ain't got no problem. Back off, buddy.*

2.) Contemplation—*Come back here, buddy. Maybe, just maybe I do have an issue. So what?*

3.) Preparation—*Enough is enough. I know what I have to do, and I am planning on making this change next Thursday morning. Bring it on!*

4.) Action—*Hiiii-yaaaaa! Check me out! I'm actually changing.*

5.) Maintenance—*Ewwwww, boyyyyy! This is kinda tricky, but I'm gonna keep at it.*

6.) Termination—*I'm pretty sure I've nailed it, but I'm still going to keep a lookout for triggers.*

Conclusion

If there is something about your life that you want to improve, change is the only option. It's that simple. There is nothing else in this universe that will help you become the person you want to be.

The truth is—and this has been researched—the average successful self-changer makes several attempts to change before achieving results. They move forward, then backward, then forward, then backward, then forward, then forward, then forward, then backward, then forward again. Get it? It's probable you will go back and forth between precontemplation, contemplation, preparation and action a bunch of times (like the Q-Bert game) before you are able to successfully change and overcome your problem.

I'm not bringing you bad news here, people, I'm just helping your mental preparation for what's to come. I want to make sure that when you do slip and end up back in stage one or two or three, you do not see it as a failure, and instead are able to lift up that glorious head of yours and reflect so you can learn something. Eventually, if you find that you are trapped in a cycle and completing stages 1, 2, 3, 4, then 3, 2, 1, 4, then 1, 2, 3, 4, then 4, 3, 2, 1, then 1, 4, 2, 3, then 1, 3, 4, 2, then, 4, 2, 1, 3 again and again, then guess what? You are not learning.

I have patience and tons of empathy for pretty much all people (unless you cause undue harm to a person or animal), but at some point all that positive regard turns into enabling if you're not able to say, "Seriously, cut the shit and stop blowing it," to a person who is not learning and appears to be going through the same motions perpetually.

There is a saying in my field that captures all of what I am trying to pile-drive into you here:

"If you keep doing what you've always done, you're going to get what you've always gotten."

If you keep acting in unhealthy ways, you will be unhealthy. If you keep thinking shitty things about yourself, you will feel shitty. If you keep complaining about the same stinky thing and don't try to change it, guess what, dingus? It won't get any better. Sorry, you're not a total dingus, but the part of you or me or anyone else that works against us and foils our success is.

Let the six stages of change help you decipher where you're at when you make the final decision regarding a real effort to improve some aspect of your life. You will find that the more you practice moving through these stages with increased self-awareness, self-management skills, and commitment, the easier it will be to go forward. Hold yourself accountable, but make sure you are being patient and gentle with yourself. This is the recipe for success. And before you know it, you will be getting rad and staying rad.

SUMMARY

Way to go! You made it through the whole book? Well, technically I don't know if you did or not, but let's give my ego a stroke here and assume you did. I know there was a lot of information in this baby, so I want to break it down for you once more. Here's everything condensed into one sexy little hairless nut.

In essence, this book was designed to give you a bunch of basic information that, once understood and applied, would help you become more of the person you want to be. To accomplish this, we went down memory lane as you thought about your young life and analyzed the attachments you formed. You realized that the environment you grew up in had a powerful effect on you, because this is where you first learned about love, safety, and distress. This all influenced the way you felt about yourself and other people as you grew up, and it affected the way you learned to manage your emotions and stress. A Get Rad principle you learned was that despite the upbringing you had and the attachments you formed with primary caregivers, you are not at the mercy of your past and it doesn't have to poison your future. As an adult, you can trade in old and junky ways of being for new and improved ones if you can change some of the negative thoughts, feelings, habits, and behaviors you have. A shit childhood does not = a shit adult life.

Then you figured out that one reason you feel like a turd sometimes is that you experience things on an emotional basis before your ability to be rational kicks in. You called yourself out and learned what you need to do to stop the crap thoughts you have that feed depressed moods, so you can pick yourself up when you're down and feel better longer. A Get Rad principle you learned is that your thoughts create your reality, and you do in fact have the power to take control of the way you interpret and experience what happens to you in life.

Then we talked about that pesky bugger, anxiety, and you were shown that it's not really meant to be pesky, and instead serves a good purpose. You learned that anxiety exists as a means of self-protection, but that in our modern world, it can get triggered by a lot by things, factors, topics, situations, and people that aren't in fact threatening to you or your survival. So you came to terms with the notion that if you're going to learn to manage anxiety and other uncomfortable feelings that make your stomach feel like there are ninja death stars flying around in there, then ya gotta make friends with them. You learned another Get Rad principle: that you can overcome anxiety if you are open to experiencing the totality of your emotions.

In the second half, you got some practical tools that can be applied to your life in order to improve the way you cope and manage your emotions, feelings, and behaviors. You learned that being self-aware means (1) you're able to examine your behavior, habits, and tendencies, while at the same time, you (2) identify the thoughts and emotions that are connected to those responses. Learning how to perceive your emotions as they occur in real time, and understanding your general pattern of behavior and how you tend to react are the two biggest components of self-awareness. You found that not treating emotions as only good or bad, paying attention to the ripple effect your emotions have, leaning into discomfort, feeling the physical aspects of your emotions, knowing what pushes your buttons, not letting a bad mood get the best of you, asking what compels you to do the things you do, and getting feedback from others are all cost-free and effective tools that you have at your disposal to help you increase your self-awareness. A Get Rad principle you learned here is that when you are self-aware, you are in control of your consciousness.

Once you nailed self-awareness to the wall, you learned about self-management, which works to help you balance out your increased awareness. Self-management, which refers to a person's ability to tune in to their emotions, is super important because it gives a person the ability to make active decisions about what they say and how they react. Tips to help you unleash this awesome power include the simple acts of conscious breathing, counting to 10, smiling and laughing, controlling your self-talk, visualizing yourself succeeding, and taking something positive away from even shit people and situations. You came to see that remaining emotionally aware and flexible in the circumstances you experience means that you are engaging in successful self-management. A Get Rad principle you learned here is that while you cannot always control what happens to you, you can control the way you allow yourself to react to it.

Last, we talked about change, why it's so damn important, and what the actual process looks like in all of us. We identified what goes on inside our head, and talked about some of the factors that we may not even be fully aware of, that go on around us and help us bust a move to make the changes we want. Then we outlined the six stages people pass through as they change: precontemplation, contemplation, preparation, action, maintenance, and termination, and saw that sometimes folks can get stuck at one or more stages or relapse, and that the successful graduation from one stage does not automatically propel you to the next. You learned it's important to put forth a genuine effort when you decide to make a change, and that moving backwards is okay and a normal part of the process. A final Get Rad principle you learned is that if you try and are unsuccessful at achieving the change you want, it's best if you do not label it as a failure. Instead, allow your effort to reinforce your continued desire to keep on keeping on. You'll get there if you keep at it, and every attempt you make makes you stronger and gets you closer to that goal.

Farewell for now, friend

And so our journey comes to an end. I'm sad to see you go! We've bonded. In between the butt, vomit and poop jokes, you let me into your world so you could learn some things about yourself to improve your life, be happier, and be more of the person you want to be.

This book was intended to help you learn about yourself so you could enhance the overall quality of your living. This is important, because you matter. I'm not sure how many lives we get once we leave this one, but in this lifetime, I believe we only get a finite number of breaths and heartbeats. Spending them miserable, unhappy, and unfulfilled is a waste, and you deserve better. The reality is that you have the power to change.

Personal growth is a process that requires practice, and every single day you have numerous opportunities to do this. To practice reframing dispiriting thoughts, to practice being mindful, to practice tolerating anxiety and distress, and to practice making a change for the better. Living fulfilled, happy, and in contentment is within your reach. Anyone can do it. It's okay if your childhood wasn't the most stable, if your family isn't ideal, if your current circumstance is stressful, or if you're not rich and famous. You are still capable of achieving the goals you desire and the dreams you hold. You are capable of creating meaning in your life. You are capable of leading your own destiny.

You are AWESOME.

You are AMAZING.

You deserve to be HAPPY.

You deserve LOVE.

You have POWER.

You can take CONTROL.

You are CAPABLE of being the person you want to be.

You can make a CHANGE.

You have a PURPOSE.

YOU DESERVE GOOD THINGS.

YOU ARE WORTHY.

YOU ARE PRECIOUS.

YOU ARE BEAUTIFUL TO BEHOLD.
Go get em, tiger.

Thank you for reading my book! Peace!!

YOU ARE AWESOME

NOTES

CHAPTER 1

1.) Mary Ainsworth was a developmental psychologist who studied attachment. She worked alongside pioneer John Bowlby researching infant-mother attachments, and later created an assessment tool to measure attachment style. Mary D. Salter Ainsworth et al., *Patterns of Attachment: A Psychological Study of the Strange Situation* (Hillsdale, New Jersey: Erlbaum, 1978).

2.) Rachel E. Dinero et al., "Influence of family of origin and adult romantic partners on romantic attachment security," *Journal of Family Psychology* 22, no. 4 (2008): 622-32.

3.) Travis Bradberry and Jean Greaves, *Emotional Intelligence 2.0* (San Diego: TalentSmart, 2009).

4.) Mary Ainsworth outlined 3 main types of attachment patterns: secure, insecure-avoidant, and insecure-ambivalent. Later the idea of a disorganized attachment style was introduced and many consider it to be a fourth type of attachment. Ainsworth created a study known as the "Strange Situation," where she observed infants and toddlers between the ages of 12 and 18 months and studied their responses after being briefly left alone then reunited with their mothers. Mary D. Salter Ainsworth and S. M. Bell, "Attachment, exploration, and separation: Illustrated by the behavior of one-year-olds in a strange situation," *Child Development 41* (1970): 49-67.

5.) Jeffrey A. Simpson et al., "Attachment and the experience and expression of emotions in romantic relationships: A developmental perspective," *Journal of Personality and Social Psychology 92*, no. 2 (2007): 355-67.

6.) Patricia M. Crittenden and Mary D. S. Ainsworth, "Child maltreatment and attachment theory," in *Child Maltreatment: Theory and Research on the Causes and Consequences of Child Abuse and Neglect,* eds. Dante Cicchetti and Vicki Carlson (New York: Cambridge University Press, 1989), 432-63.

CHAPTER 2

1.) American Psychiatric Association, *Diagnostic and Statistical Manual of Mental Disorders*, 5th ed. (Arlington, Virginia: American Psychiatric Publishing, 2013).

2.) Ibid. The DSM suggests that having five of the nine symptoms meets criteria that could lead to a diagnosis of a major depressive episode. My own opinion is that having four of the nine criteria listed is grounds for seeking psychological treatment.

3.) Dr. Aaron T. Beck is considered to be the founding father of cognitive therapy (1960), which is a form of treatment designed to help individuals identify and then alter negative thoughts that keep them depressed. Dr. Beck coined the term "automatic thoughts" to describe the negative cognitions depressed individuals often have. Aaron T. Beck at al., *Cognitive Therapy of Depression* (New York: The Guilford Press, 1979). Dr. Daniel Amen has also made significant contributions to the field of depression, and has extensively studied brain disorders. The idea of Automatic Negative Thoughts is attributed to Dr. Amen. He discusses this topic at length in his book Change Your Brain, Change Your Life (New York: Three Rivers Press, 1998).

4.) Amen, *Change Your Brain*. Georgia A. DeGangi, *The Dysregulated Adult: Integrated Treatment Approaches* (London: Academic Press, 2012).

5.) Amen, Change Your Brain. Datis Kharrazian, *Why isn't my Brain Working?* (Carlsbad, CA: Elephant Press, 2013).

6.) Travis Bradberry and Jean Greaves, *Emotional Intelligence 2.0* (San Diego: TalentSmart, 2009).

7.) Amen, *Change Your Brain*. DeGangi, *The Dysregulated Adult*.

8.) Amen, *Change Your Brain*. Kharrazian, *Why isn't my Brain Working?*

CHAPTER 3

1.) Aaron T. Beck, A. John Rush, Brian F. Shaw, and Gary Emery, *Cognitive Therapy of Depression* (New York: The Guilford Press, 1979). Albert Ellis, *Overcoming Destructive Beliefs, Feelings and Behaviors: New Directions for Rational Emotive Behavior Therapy* (New York: Prometheus Books, 2001). David D. Burns, *The Feeling Good Handbook* (New York: Penguin Group, 1999).

2.) David D. Burns, *The Feeling Good Handbook* (New York: Penguin Group, 1999). Aaron T. Beck et al., *Cognitive Therapy of Depression* (New York: The Guilford Press, 1979).

3.) Mihaly Csikszentmihalyi, *Flow: The Psychology of Optimal Experience* (New York: Harper Collins, 1990).

4.) Ibid, pg 2.

5.) Ibid.

CHAPTER 4

1.) Acceptance and commitment therapy was developed in the 1980s and purports that cognitive flexibility can be increased when acceptance strategies are used in combination with commitment and behavior-change strategies. Steven C. Hayes et al., *Acceptance and Commitment Therapy: An Experiential Approach to Behavior Change* (New York: Guilford Press, 1999).

2.) Georg H. Eifert and John P. Forsyth, *Acceptance and Commitment Therapy for Anxiety Disorders: A Practitioner's Treatment Guide to Using Mindfulness, Acceptance, and Values-Based Behavior Change Strategies* (Oakland, CA: New Harbinger Publications, 2005).

3.) Veronique Mead, "The sympathetic nervous system," accessed September 16, 2012, http:www.Veroniquemead.com.

4.) Eifert and Forsyth, *Acceptance and Commitment Therapy for Anxiety Disorders.*

5.) Dennis D. Tirch, *The Compassionate-Mind Guide to Overcoming Anxiety: Using Compassion-Focused Therapy to Calm Worry, Panic, and Fear* (Oakland, CA: New Harbinger Publications, 2012).

CHAPTER 5

1.) Georg H. Eifert and John P. Forsyth, *Acceptance and Commitment Therapy for Anxiety Disorders: A Practitioner's Treatment Guide to Using Mindfulness, Acceptance, and Values-Based Behavior Change Strategies* (Oakland, CA: New Harbinger Publications, 2005). Dennis D. Tirch, *The Compassionate-Mind Guide to Overcoming Anxiety: Using Compassion-Focused Therapy to Calm Worry, Panic, and Fear* (Oakland, CA: NewHarbinger Publications, 2012).

2.) Eifert and Forsyth, *Acceptance and Commitment Therapy for Anxiety Disorders.* Pg 39.

3.) Ibid, pg 39.

4.) Tirch, *The Compassionate-Mind Guide.*
Jon Kabat-Zinn, *Wherever You Go, There You Are: Mindfulness Meditation in Everyday Life* (New York: Hyperion, 1994). Jon Kabat-Zinn, *Coming to Our Senses: Healing Ourselves and the World Through Mindfulness* (New York: Piatkus, 2005).

5.) Elizabeth Kubler-Ross, *On Death and Dying* (New York: Scribner, 1969).

CHAPTER 6

1.) In their book, *Emotional Intelligence 2.0,* Travis Bradberry and Jean Greaves discuss how people can develop their self-awareness, self-management, social awareness, and relationship management skills in order to improve their quality of life. The principles they outline are cited throughout this chapter. Travis Bradberry and Jean

Greaves, Emotional Intelligence 2.0 (San Diego: TalentSmart, 2009)

2.) David L. Forbes, "Toward a unified model of human motivation," *Review of General Psychology* 15, no. 2 (2011), 85-98.
Sheldon, K.M and Schuler, J. "Wanting, having, and needing: Integrating motive disposition theory and self-determination theory." Journal of Personality and Social Psychology 101, no. 5 (2012): 1106-23.

3.) Edward L. Deci and Richard M. Ryan, Intrinsic Motivation and Self-Determination in Human Behavior (New York: Plenum Press, 1985).
Edward Deci and Richard M. Ryan, "The 'what' and 'why' of goal pursuits: Human needs and the self-determination of behavior," *Psychological Inquiry* 11 (2000): 227-268.
Edward L. Deci and Richard M. Ryan, "Facilitating optimal motivation and psychological well-being across life's domains," *Canadian Psychology*, 49(1): 14-23.

CHAPTER 7

1.) Travis Bradberry and Jean Greaves, *Emotional Intelligence 2.0* (San Diego: TalentSmart, 2009).

2.) The principles listed throughout this chapter are based on the self-management strategies outlined by Travis Bradberry and Jean Greaves in their book, *Emotional Intelligence 2.0* (San Diego: TalentSmart, 2009).

3.) Bruce Davis, "There are 50,000 thoughts standing between you and your partner every day!" *The Huffington Post*, May 23, 2013, http://www. huffingtonpost.com/ bruce-davis-phd/healthy-relationships _b _3307916. html.

4.) "Your lungs," American Lung Association, (2014), http://www.lung.org/ your-lungs/.

5.) "Cut to the heart," Nova Online, (1997), http://www.pbs.org/wgbh/nova/ heart/heartfacts.html.

6.) Merrimack   Vision   Care,   April   25,   2013, http://www.merrimackvision.com/blog/topics/blinking-facts/.

7.) Travis Bradberry and Jean Greaves, *Emotional Intelligence 2.0* (San Diego: TalentSmart, 2009). Srinivasan Pillay, "The science of visualization: Maximizing your brain's potential during the recession," *The Huffington Post,* March 3, 2009, http://www.huffingtonpost.com/srinivasan-pillay/the-science-of-visualizat_ b_ 171340.html.

8.) E. J. Masicampo and Roy F. Baumeister, "Consider it done! Plan-making can eliminate the cognitive effects of unfulfilled goals," *Journal of Personality and Social Psychology* 101 no. 4 (2001): 667-83. Peter M. Gollwitzer, "Implementation intentions: Strong effects of simple plans," *American Psychologist* 54 (1999): 493-503.

9.) Travis Bradberry and Jean Greaves, *Emotional Intelligence 2.0* (San Diego: TalentSmart, 2009).

CHAPTER 8

1.) James O. Prochaska, John C. Norcross, and Carlo C. DiClemente are experts in the field of self-change. They have extensively researched and written about this topic, and the nine processes that facilitate and support change discussed in this chapter are based upon their collective work and the data they originally published. James O. Prochaska, John C. Norcross, and Carlo C. DiClemente, *Changing for Good: A Revolutionary Six-Stage Program for Overcoming Bad Habits and Moving your Life Positively Forward* (New York: HarperCollins, 1994).

CHAPTER 9

1.) James O. Prochaska, John C. Norcross, and Carlo C. DiClemente, *Changing for Good: A Revolutionary Six-Stage Program for Overcoming Bad Habits and Moving Your Life Positively Forward* (New York: HarperCollins, 1994), pg. 37.

2.) The six stages of change were first developed by psychologists James O. Prochaska, John C. Norcross, and Carlo C. DiClemente. The stages discussed in this chapter are based upon their collective work and the data they originally published. Prochaska, Norcross, and DiClemente, Changing for Good.

order at www.pegasusbooks.net

* 9 7 8 1 9 4 1 8 5 9 3 3 9 *